QUANTUM JOURNEYS

I0560359

Tales of Multidimensional Healing and Discovery

Second Edition

Kryssa Marie Bowman

In loving memory of Shepherd Dobson

1972-2022

Table of Contents

Foreword:

In the realm of healing and transformation, the mind, body, and spirit converge in a symphony of discovery, resilience, and profound change. As I delve into the pages of "Quantum Journeys Hypnosis," I am reminded of the boundless potential within each of us to transcend the ordinary and embrace the extraordinary.

Kryssa Marie Bowman's work stands as a testament to this potential, offering a beacon of hope and a roadmap for those seeking to unlock the deeper dimensions of their consciousness. This is something that she and I share as esteemed colleagues: the discovery of the truth utilizing uncommon and more esoteric techniques.

The journey into Quantum Journeys Hypnosis (QJH) is not merely a foray into traditional hypnotherapy; it is an exploration into the multidimensional nature of our existence. Here, Bowman masterfully integrates principles of neuroscience, quantum physics, and metaphysical wisdom to create a holistic healing modality that speaks to both skeptics and believers alike. Through the lens of QJH, we are invited to witness the miraculous transformations of individuals who have dared to confront their deepest fears, uncover past lives, meet spirit guides, and even visit the Akashic Records.

Each chapter of this book serves as a portal into the myriad experiences of clients who have walked the path of QJH. From an atheist communicating with a higher power to the resolution of deep-seated traumas and phobias, the stories shared within these pages are as diverse as they are enlightening. Bowman's approach is rooted in a deep respect for the individual journey, allowing each client's Highest-Self to guide the session, free from judgment and preconceived notions.

What sets this work apart is Bowman's willingness to embrace curiosity over confidence. Her journey from traditional hypnotherapy to the development of QJH is a narrative of surrendering to the unknown, of setting aside personal preferences to honor the experiences and wisdom of her clients. This humility and openness have paved the way for groundbreaking insights and healing techniques that resonate on a soul level.

The science of consciousness, as Bowman illustrates, is a frontier that blends the tangible with the intangible, the seen with the unseen. It challenges us to expand our understanding of reality and to acknowledge the interconnectedness of all things. By weaving together scientific exploration and spiritual discovery, "Quantum Journeys Hypnosis" offers a comprehensive guide to navigating the complexities of the human experience.

As you journey through the pages of Bowman's work, I encourage you to open your mind and heart to the possibilities presented. Whether you are a seasoned practitioner, a curious skeptic, or someone seeking personal transformation, there is wisdom here for you. Let this book be a companion on your path to greater awareness, healing, and connection with your Highest-Self.

In the spirit of exploration and healing,

Stephanie C. Conkle

Clinical Hypnotherapist

June 16, 2024.

Introduction:

For the purposes of this book, all references to God, Source, Angels, Archangels, ETs, etc., are the client's own language and are not indicative of my personal beliefs. My beliefs are not relevant to my sessions, and I teach this to my students as well.

I intend to explore the relationship we have with our multidimensional consciousness and strengthen it through open communication. Being aware of, or having knowledge of, these other aspects, including our subconscious mind, our higher consciousness, etc., is not the same as having an actual relationship with them. Coming to know them, working with them, befriending them, and embodying them changes a person's life in incredibly profound and permanent ways. Once you come to know aspects of your higher consciousness, you can't ever not know them again.

About Quantum Journeys Hypnosis™ and Kryssa Marie Bowman

Quantum Journeys Hypnosis™ (QJH) helps you gain a deep understanding of the mind–body–spirit connection and how to use it to overcome a wide range of challenges, from anxiety and phobias to chronic pain, weight management, and motivation.

What sets Quantum Journeys Hypnosis apart from other, more traditional forms of hypnosis is that we take a multidimensional approach, which means we are not just working with the subconscious mind. We are also working with the client's highest consciousness, sometimes called the Higher-self or superconscious mind, as well as the consciousness of their physical body. We do this by combining elements of neuroscience, principles of quantum physics, and expanded states of awareness.

This process allows QJH™ clients to access past lives, meet spirit guides, communicate with their inner healer, design and orchestrate quantum jumps, and even visit the Akashic Records while resting in a deep state of trance.

When I first ventured into hypnotherapy, I had no intention of exploring spiritual hypnosis. I had experienced my own metaphysical encounters, but because I was conflicted about them, I intended to stick with strictly clinical hypnosis. However, there were apparently other plans in store for me that I was not yet aware of at the time.

It is also worth noting that I carried a fair amount of anxiety and imposter syndrome in those first couple of years as a professional hypnotist, not only because I was new to the field, but also because my first instructors trained me to believe that my confidence "ran the show" of a session. They taught that if I was not in a highly confident ego state, I should essentially fake it, since on some level, hypnosis is similar to a placebo: the client believes they can achieve results, and because of this belief, they do.

While there is a kernel of truth in that, it is not the only truth, and it felt out of alignment with my deeper values. I was not interested in faking it until I made it. It was not that I could not do it—it was that I found it exhausting. In fact, it made me dread going to work.

So, when my clients began channeling their higher consciousness within their sessions, I had to choose between setting my personal preferences aside and remaining open to whatever their experiences were, or corralling them back to the clinical hypnosis I had intended for them. The latter would effectively invalidate their experiences and potentially set them back in their own evolution.

The only choice I knew I could live with was to set aside my preferences and let my clients have their experiences free of judgment, free of corralling, and free of invalidation.

This required an entirely new approach to hypnotherapy. Rather than pretending to be confident, I fully embraced being curious. And you know what? It worked out better than I ever could have imagined!

I entered each session with pure curiosity, wondering what might happen if I let my client's higher consciousness lead the way rather than my ego. If I handed the steering wheel to the part of my clients that had access to all the wisdom, knowledge, and healing they needed, then it would take some of the pressure off me. I simply needed to facilitate the conversation they had with those aspects of their consciousness that knew how best to help them.

And this is where things became truly interesting. I found myself going into mild trance states right along with my clients, receiving suggestions and tips from my own higher consciousness on how to best proceed. Since I recorded all of my sessions (with the client's permission), I was able to listen later and take notes on what we did, their responses, and their outcomes. These suggestions became the foundation for the Quantum Journeys Hypnosis protocol, and because they came through my own higher consciousness, I have always considered them a gift.

In October 2021, I had a conversation with an aspect of my higher consciousness that goes by the name of EL. This aspect holds both feminine and masculine energy, though leaning slightly feminine, so I sometimes use she/her and sometimes they/them pronouns. EL challenged me to follow every suggestion given for one full year to deepen my connection, strengthen my intuition, and establish greater trust in myself and in life.

EL said my life would be unrecognizable in a year and that it would be best not to set specific goals or follow external steps toward achievements, but to instead surrender to intuition. To trust.

At the time, I was lonely. My children were grown, and we had moved into separate living situations. I had no partner—though always cats—and I was broke beyond broke. So I agreed. I figured whatever changes my higher consciousness suggested could only improve my life.

I first consciously met EL in the spring of 2021 in a trade session with a woman I had studied regression-to-cause hypnotherapy with. I later realized I had met EL during a Near-Death Experience, though I did not recall her name at that time. My colleague guided me into trance, and soon our session was hijacked by EL, speaking through me in direct voice. EL began speaking directly through me. Some call this channeling.

This surprised us both, as I had never considered myself a channeler, and she had never encountered anything like it. Sadly, this was more than she was comfortable with, and over the next month, she made it clear she no longer wanted to work with me. I was sad to lose her after we had become so close, but EL assured me this was the nature of stepping into a different frequency. Some people naturally fall away, and others are naturally drawn in, like a magnet attracting and repelling depending on the match.

At first, this stirred up ancient rejection and abandonment wounds. But even that turned out to be for the best, because I needed to process and heal them. And the only way to heal them was to feel them. It is impossible to heal something unless it is present. Imagine trying to heal a headache years later, or a sprained ankle before it even happens—you just cannot. So I wished her well and accepted that life might grow lonelier for a time, but that this was part of healing. I did my best to surrender to it.

In December, I received a clear message from EL about starting an online healing group. I was to invite everyone I thought might resonate and not worry about the particulars—namely, that I had no idea how to facilitate an online group. I was assured I would receive instructions on an as-needed basis and that if I built it, they would come.

My friend Liliana Myers resonated with this and referred me to another woman who had been facilitating healing groups and had published books on the subject, Dr. Lynne McTaggart. She was a scientist and researcher whose initial experiments with intention were designed to disprove the possibility that a group of people could affect someone or something at a distance. Yet her results showed the opposite.

> *"To be a true explorer is to carry on your exploration, even if it takes you to a place you didn't particularly plan to go to."*
> ~ Lynne McTaggart

My mission differed from McTaggart's in that I was not seeking to prove or disprove anything. I simply wanted to bring together those who felt called to participate and keep an open mind about the results. Primarily, it was about experiencing the collective energy and shared consciousness. This experience, in turn, could act as a permission slip for everyone involved, allowing us to request and receive healing for ourselves by first offering it to others.

Anyone familiar with the healing arts, whether alternative or allopathic, knows there is often a strong desire to focus on others rather than the self. Many feel there is something wrong with them if they cannot heal themselves, so they focus outward instead. It feels safer and less vulnerable than asking for or accepting help.

From the very start, my goal was to open channels of healing for others, since that was the more comfortable route. By doing so, it became easier to realize that we serve others best when we also allow ourselves to receive. Ultimately, this helps us manifest our own best lives.

There is a strange paradox in believing we are unworthy of receiving help, yet fully willing to offer it. As Brené Brown has pointed out, if we judge ourselves as inferior for needing help, then we also, without meaning to, judge those we help as inferior.

This belief is not helpful when your life's work is to serve others. It positions the practitioner as somehow superior, which can feed the ego in damaging ways and does not serve the client.

But I digress. The point was that EL suggested I create this healing group, even though I had no idea how. The group grew almost entirely by word-of-mouth. Some joined only to manifest their best lives and left when they grew bored of sending healing intentions. Others wanted to give but not receive, and eventually dropped away. Some wanted to receive without giving and either left or stayed until they were ready to reciprocate. Still others dropped in sporadically, while a few showed up week after week to both give and receive.

Of those who stayed, fascinating things occurred. At first, many were hesitant to share their experiences after sending healing intentions. They often began with disclaimers like, "I don't know if this makes sense, but…" and then discovered that others had received nearly identical impressions. Over time, participants grew more trusting of their inner wisdom, more willing to share openly, and more confident in their intuition. Their lives began to change in remarkable ways.

This experiment proved deeply successful. It also taught me that it is natural for people to come and go, and it is important not to let the ego invalidate them for joining or leaving. Some may have left because I was not the right facilitator for them, and that was okay. In the pursuit of alignment, it is just as valuable to discover what does not fit as what does.

Recipients of our group healing reported incredible results. Not everyone experienced complete healing, but most felt more at peace, more supported, and surrounded by compassion. Some found new perspectives on their challenges. I will share more about this global healing group, which now includes participants from all over the world, in a future book.

After this process, EL tasked me with gathering the insights from the group, along with my one-to-one hypnotherapy sessions, my academic background in biopsychology and neuroscience, and the channeled messages I was receiving, to create a class that would teach others how to communicate directly with higher consciousness.

At first, this seemed overwhelming. My ego whispered, "Who are you to teach this? You are a newbie. No one will listen." These thoughts, rooted in self-doubt, were just trying to keep me safe from ridicule. But EL said they were not asking for much—just one class. A class to help colleagues guide clients into trance states where they could connect with their Higher-self for positive regression. This was more empowering than working only with the protective subconscious. After a battle with my ego, I agreed.

I was not sure anyone would sign up. To comfort myself, I decided that if fewer than eight people registered, I would refund them and retreat to my comfort zone. To my surprise, about twenty professionals enrolled. Since then, over five hundred people have purchased the replay, available on my website. The class, Tapping into the Higher-self for Positive Hypnotic Regression, became the seed of Quantum Journeys Hypnosis.

What happened next was miraculous. I discovered that although I was uncomfortable in crowds, I felt completely at ease in the role of teacher. I could feel the energy of the students, and I knew instinctively to honor that exchange. I realized that there are teachers who harvest the energy of their students for their own gain, and teachers who share the energy for the benefit of all. I was relieved to find myself in the latter camp.

The energy exchange was equal, like breathing. I could not take without giving, and I could give without receiving. It was a beautiful symbiosis that erased my fear of teaching. Anyone who judged me was simply not my tribe. And that was okay.

This did not mean I was one hundred percent confident. I doubt I ever will be. My guidance came from my Higher-self, but I am no more or less divine than any other human being. I have an ego, and egos are part of being human. They protect us, guide us, and challenge us. But we all also have a Higher-self— the part that loves us unconditionally and wants our best.

Our Higher-self was there when we were born, reminding us that it would be okay despite the chaos. It was there when we first learned to crawl and walk, cheering us on rather than criticizing us for falling. It was there when we discovered joy in running, dancing, and playing, even if our ego later whispered that we were not good enough.

The subconscious mind is designed to keep us alive, not necessarily to make us happy. It repeats whatever it learned in order to protect us. And it extends this protection not only to threats against our body, but also to threats against our sense of identity. It teaches us to "fit in," which is often the opposite of true belonging.

Those with neurodivergent minds know this deeply.

What we can learn is that every person has a Higher-self offering reminders that life is worth it. Sadly, some lose touch with that guidance and come to see the world only as threatening. When that happens, life becomes lonely and painful.

I have lost loved ones to suicide and addiction, and I myself struggled with suicidal thoughts at thirteen, eighteen, and thirty-two. My childhood trauma, my Near-Death Experience, and even medication side effects all contributed. For decades, I carried one foot out the door.

This was the seed of my agoraphobia in my thirties and forties, worsened by a stalker and an abusive marriage. I was diagnosed with PTSD and generalized anxiety. I truly went through hell to get where I am today.

Looking back, I now know that what kept me alive was my Higher-self. She loved me. She encouraged me not to judge myself harshly. She reminded me that escaping early would only pass unresolved trauma to the next generation.

In later sessions, I discovered past life experiences where I had used trance for vision quests and healing. When I asked if I could bring forward that wisdom, I received an emphatic yes, along with joy that I had figured it out. My Higher-self made clear that starting over each lifetime only delayed the real work.

From there, everything accelerated. EL gave me clear steps to strengthen my channels of connection:

1. Start each day with 20–30 minutes of meditation, self-hypnosis, or hemi-sync recordings, taking advantage of liminal brain wave states in the morning.

2. Watch the sunrise or spend at least 20 minutes in direct morning sunlight to set the Reticular Activating System to seek joy and beauty.

3. Open channels with the physical body. Move, stretch, or roll on a yoga mat until communication flows.

4. Dial the senses open to notice subtle shifts. Observe them without absorbing. Choose which messages to receive and which to release.

5. Recognize that unexpected thoughts or feelings are often not your own. Some are gifts

of creativity or intuition, while others may come from human or lower sources. You will know by whether your heart expands or contracts.

About this Book:

The title of this book will likely attract a more spiritual audience, and that's wonderful, but please know that I am also a huge fan of science and scientific research—specifically the realms of neuroscience, quantum physics, the science of consciousness, and biopsychology. My own academic background is in Applied Psychology and Gender Studies, with some emphasis on human sexuality.

There have been many books written on the subject of spiritual hypnosis, and I am not here to say that this one is better, or that it should be read instead of another, or even in any particular order. I tend to trust that our higher consciousness brings the books, classes, educators, and mentors into our lives in exactly the timing that is right for each of us.

However, there is one thing you may notice is missing from this book that often appears in the works of my predecessors: I am not interested in proving to you that there is something beyond the physical three-dimensional world that your conscious, waking mind is most familiar with. I am merely presenting the evidence.

That said, I will forewarn you—there may be a shift in your perception of reality simply from reading this book. Your analytical, conscious mind isn't the only reader here. Your subconscious will also take in this information, and other aspects of your consciousness will be aware of it as well. Elements of your own ancient knowledge, wisdom, and understanding may awaken. It is not my job to convince you of anything—it would be pointless anyway. You are wherever you are on the spectrum of belief and disbelief, and you will either allow yourself to explore more of that spectrum or you will not. Neither outcome will be the result of my persuasion.

I also hold no negative judgment toward those who doubt. In fact, I respect them greatly. The spirit of scientific exploration has always required both skeptics and visionaries. We cannot progress with only one. My personal belief is that we are in constant collaboration with our Higher Selves, whether we are aware of it or not. If someone is living a lifetime without open-mindedness, this is not an accident, nor is it my place—or my right—to convince them otherwise. We are all here for a reason, and it does not matter whether we understand each other's reasons.

My role with this anthology is to present the case studies, the session stories, the insights and epiphanies, and the verifiable, real-world results of these sessions. What you do with this information is entirely up to you.

The contributors to this anthology are my beloved students and graduates of Quantum Journeys Hypnosis, as well as a few clients. Some have been professional hypnotherapists and hypnotists for decades, while others have only my training. Some entered QJH Academy with a keen interest in what we affectionately call "woo-woo" experiences—the metaphysical and the esoteric. Others arrived with no interest in woo at all, yet felt drawn to the possibility of communicating with multidimensional consciousness.

What is Multidimensional Consciousness?

In 2022, three quantum physicists—John Clauser, Alain Aspect, and Anton Zeilinger—won the Nobel Prize for validating that reality is non-local, meaning that physical objects do not have definite properties until they are observed. This, coupled with quantum entanglement—where particles communicate instantaneously across vast, even infinite distances—has turned our understanding of reality upside down.

If reality is not merely physical and three-dimensional, then what we interact with here at the physical level is, for all intents and purposes, just the user interface our human brains can grasp. It is not the entirety of reality.

The troubling part is that we do not really know what the entirety of reality is. And even if we were to stumble upon it, I doubt we could fully comprehend it. It would be like showing trigonometry to an infant and expecting them not only to understand it but also to explain it without language skills. Nor would such comprehension serve much purpose. We are biological creatures with an imperative to survive physical life. If we could perceive every frequency available, we would be overwhelmed, even immobilized. Dysfunctional.

Instead, we are given the ability to sense only what is most necessary for survival. Some of us, however, have additional sensory abilities. The ability to perceive discarnate humans—ghosts, for example—is considered an extrasensory perception.

So, the next best thing to understanding this larger, multidimensional reality—one beyond the grasp of our primary senses—is what some members of the scientific community call the science of consciousness. University of California's Cognitive Psychologist, Donald Hoffman, is at the forefront of this. As are retired ER physician and ufologist Steven Greer, and Chris Bledsoe, author of the best-selling book UFO Of God.

The science of consciousness proposes that consciousness flows through everything and that all is connected. Or, as Arthur Schopenhauer suggested in the mid-1800s, all consciousness is ultimately a singularity, behaving as separate only when fractalized. Consider the cells of our body: our liver cells work together yet independently to cleanse and detoxify the system, while our neurons handle communication and thought. Each cell type affects the other, even though they never meet directly. Both originated from a singular source: DNA. That DNA serves as the singularity, the source code running through every cell.

We already know a great deal about frequencies of light and sound, and exciting new research explores olfactory frequencies. It turns out that the way we perceive smell is closer to the way we hear sound—specific aromatic "notes" pluck at receptors tuned to them, much like musical frequencies.

What we also know, without question, is that humans are severely limited in sensory perception compared to other mammals.

Humans can only see about 0.0035% of the electromagnetic spectrum—the detectable light range. That tiny slice corresponds to the rainbow of colors from 380 to 750 nanometers. And yet, many people refuse to believe what they cannot see, despite not seeing much at all.

We are equally limited in hearing. The human range is roughly 20 Hz to 20 kHz. Infants can hear slightly above 20 kHz, but most adults drop closer to 15–17 kHz. Frequencies below 20 Hz are infrasonic, and those above 20,000 Hz are ultrasonic.

So, there exists a massive range of frequencies beyond what we can perceive—and yet they still affect us.

Black Ops have been rumored to use inaudible sound to cause cellular damage. Horror and suspense films are known to employ sub-audible frequencies to induce unease. It stands to reason that some people are naturally more sensitive to these unseen ranges. Those who claim to see or hear transdimensional, interdimensional, or multidimensional beings would be considered to have extrasensory perception—ESP.

Tragically, people with these sensitivities are rarely celebrated. More often, they are dismissed, invalidated, ridiculed, or even persecuted. Subconsciously, many end up turning those senses down or off altogether for survival.

But in trance or deep meditation, we gain access to broader sensory abilities because we are no longer limited to our physical senses. Through imagination, we can tap into this greater consciousness. Imagination is not the opposite of reality—it is the doorway to it.

The CIA has known this for decades. The Monroe Institute's Gateway Program was used to train certain agents to astral travel—also called remote viewing—

by inducing trance and working through the imagination, assisted by brainwave synchronization. They called it Hemi-Sync.

So not only is imagination not opposed to reality, it is, as quantum physics has shown through non-locality, the very creator of reality. Through altered states—brain waves operating below Alpha—we can communicate with the multidimensionality of consciousness, from the microscopic levels of DNA to the planetary consciousness of Earth… and beyond.

For the Skeptics:

My personal opinion is that people who unquestioningly *disbelieve* unexplainable phenomena are just as narrow-minded as people who unquestioningly *believe* all of it without question. It's better to be skeptical and simply keep an open mind to the experiences, isn't it?

My work with people often results in them exploring other lifetimes, quantum jumping in this lifetime, meeting spirit guides and angelic beings, releasing entity attachments, and visiting the Akashic Records...but I don't "believe" or "disbelieve" these experiences because they are not contingent upon my faith.

My job isn't to believe, disbelieve, have faith in, or debunk; it is merely to facilitate and record the experiences. What they or you choose to do with the information and seemingly miraculous recoveries and transformations is not up to me. It's really none of my business, nor could I possibly have any control over how you'll interpret them.

It wouldn't serve my clients' highest good for me to push my own personal agenda on them or interpret their experiences for them. Nor would it serve me to form some steadfast belief in something here because the moment I do that, I become just as narrow-minded as those who steadfastly disbelieve without any research, experience, empirical evidence, or data.

Being a skeptic is a good thing. A GREAT thing actually! But many people mistake skepticism with blind disbelief.

A true skeptic has an open mind, which allows for their opinions and perceptions to be challenged and even changed. So, if you "don't believe" simply because you're unwilling to have your opinions and perceptions challenged, then please don't call yourself a skeptic.

If you're still with me, then there's a good chance you are exactly the audience for this book.

From the Practitioner's perspective

A Lonely Ego State Invites a Dark Elemental

By Kryssa Marie Bowman

A colleague of mine sent me a potential client who was hearing a voice inside his head, as she felt this was beyond her scope of practice. I was fairly certain it would be beyond my own scope of practice as well, as hypnosis is contraindicated for schizophrenia, schizoaffective disorder, and a few other mental health diagnoses. It sounded like something that a doctor of psychiatry would be better suited for, but I agreed to at least have a Discovery Call with this potential client.

During the phone call, however, I discovered that what my colleague referred to as a voice was really closer to an intrusive ego state, an introject (a strong, negative belief system picked up from someone else), or possibly even an entity attachment. What I wasn't counting on was it being all three!

I decided to take this client to The Temple of Healing, a hypnotic construct I first learned of through David Quigley, founder of Alchemical Hypnosis. With David's permission, I fleshed out the Temple of

Healing and the role of the Inner Healer that lives there and added it to the QJHA curriculum.

Upon entering his Temple of Healing, my client was immediately surrounded by winged creatures, and then, upon invitation, his Inner Healer made itself known as a large orb of white light. I asked this orb to conduct a scan of my client's physical body to look for any imbalances, abnormalities, inflammation, illness, or anything else in need of healing at the physical level.

As we got to the client's solar plexus area, he said that he "felt where something was attached" to him, and it was mostly hooked in on the left side of his body, and had tentacles reaching up to his head, down his spine, and into his solar plexus. He had been working to rid himself of this for several years. Since at least 2011, he said. When he asked what this attachment was, the answer my client received from other practitioners was that it was a dark elemental. A creature that feeds off of low emotional frequencies and typically doesn't attach directly to a person's body, but rather remains part of their emotional body.

Upon further investigation, we found that it had been invited to attach physically by an ego state that was terrified of being alone. And this ego state came with its own introject that was picked up from the client's father. The negative belief picked up from the father was that "happiness never lasts", and so the ego state claimed that it was trying to help my client to experience exactly what he expected, which was that happiness can't last, by preventing him from experiencing happiness. Except that by doing this, it had been cast out and repressed, denied, ignored, and just generally made to feel very unwelcome. So, because it was afraid of being left so all alone, it allowed for an entity attachment to keep it company in the deepest recesses of my client's subconscious…which correlates to the physical body.

As we were working out how to help heal this wounded ego state, so that it would allow the release of this entity and then send the introject back to where it came from, his higher consciousness gave him a glimpse of a past lifetime where he was a monk and made a vow to spend his life as a hermit, always alone. He then connected the pieces of how this particular fear carried forth into this lifetime and became an ego state, which some people refer to as subpersonalities, or if you're more familiar with Internal Family Systems, it would be called a Part.

We worked first with the introject, because those are the easiest to address. Then we worked with his physical body and requested his Inner Healer and the winged helpers to please begin loosening the tentacles and pulling out the energetic hook of this dark elemental. They had to do this all together, simultaneously, in order to release it. While they were busy doing this, I worked directly with my clients' wounded ego state, using some good old-fashioned logic on it until it saw how harmful it was in carrying out its job. It agreed to try a new approach to the happiness thing in exchange for an invitation to be brought back and reintegrated into my client more fully, so it wasn't so lonely and lost.

It chose its new job to be bringing a sense of childlike wonder and awe, pointing out the whimsical and magical, and beautiful aspects of life, and it decided it wanted to look like Dr. Suess's The Cat in The Hat because it missed out on having a childhood, having first been created by my clients' subconscious mind at the age of 5.

I asked his Inner Healer and Higher Consciousness to please fill in all of the newly vacated spots where the dark elemental had been living before with pure light and love so that my client's physical body wouldn't feel a sense of loss or have to grieve the departure of this entity.

At the end of the session, my client said he couldn't believe the number of epiphanies and deep insights he discovered and that he was looking forward to experiencing a renewed sense of liberation and joy in the near future.

> *I work with ego states frequently. In fact, one could build their entire hypnosis practice on just this one tool alone. It is that powerful. The version of ego state work I do and teach my students is based on Mike Mandel's Ego State Transformation, which is itself based on Gordon Emmerson's Resource States work. It's not recommended to try to get rid of an ego/resource state, as they'll just go into deeper hiding instead. We need to help them evolve, find some version of fulfilment with how they help the person, and then reintegrate them.*
>
> *Introjects are those pesky negative beliefs we pick up from other people or sometimes from circumstances. They aren't ours; they aren't trying to help us in any way, and they serve no higher purpose, so they must go whenever encountered.*

Entities may or may not be quantifiably "real", and perhaps they are merely a metaphor the subconscious mind creates in order to make symbolic sense of what is going on. It's not for me to decide.

If an entity shows up in a client session, then I help them deal with evicting it in whatever way we need to. It's not my place to invalidate their experience. When I encounter entities in a session, they are usually just lost souls or discarnated humans, according to my client's highest consciousness. But not always.

Every once in a while, I'll come across something else, like this dark elemental. What is a dark elemental? Well, I'm not altogether sure. But that doesn't prevent me from helping my client get rid of it. And in the end, if the client feels liberated from the issue, then that is all that matters. Not whether or not anyone can prove or disprove the existence of whatever happens to show up in these sessions.

~Kryssa

A Tiny Entity Attachment Causing Major Disturbances

By Kryssa Marie Bowman

A client called me asking for help with weight loss. This is one of the things hypnosis is famous for, and I've had quite a bit of experience in this field. I used to run a 12-week weight loss and body image recovery program, so I felt pretty good about accepting this client.

We went through the usual questions regarding when she last felt she was at her ideal weight, and whether she was happy with her body at that time, or if she still managed to find things to dislike about it. I asked her about the patterns of her eating and the emotions associated with food, with the consumption of said food, and with her body before, during, and after eating. We examined the cycle of shame and guilt she felt stuck in and determined what her goals were with both food and body image.

Our session was online only as she lived in a different part of the world, and when we revisited her intake at the beginning of her session, she disclosed that she'd had a late-stage miscarriage and every time she would lose any amount of weight, she'd gain it back again and be at exactly the weight she was when she'd miscarried. She felt that this had become her reset.

I questioned how she felt about that miscarriage and about her grieving process. She said she never really felt like she had the time or energy to properly grieve because she was raising two young children already. She also said that her doctor had determined that the scarring left behind from the D&C procedure following that miscarriage, which happened at 30 weeks of gestation, would likely prevent her from carrying another pregnancy to full term. So, for health reasons, she was placed on birth control implants to prevent future insemination. This didn't sit well, as she really wanted another baby. So, we decided to visit her Temple of Healing to meet and work with her Inner Healer as the first stop on her Quantum Journey.

After inducing a trance and establishing a connection with her highest consciousness, we went to her Temple and met her Inner Healer, who appeared as a Greek Goddess named Cynthia. (*side note: I've encountered "Cynthia" in several sessions since this one). I asked Cynthia to please do three body scans, beginning with physical.

My client said her entire pelvic region and lower back became very warm when Cynthia reached that part of her body. Cynthia shared with her that there was an imbalance in her womb and that she was working to bring balance, but that the source was at an emotional level. So, when we completed the rest of my client's physical body scan, where there were a handful of other imbalances brought up and easily resolved (a sluggish thyroid, pain in her left shoulder, and something in her right knee from an old injury), I asked Cynthia to please perform an emotional body scan.

The emotional body is part of the physical body and it's the job of the subconscious mind to protect both, so when an emotional trauma is either too great to handle with the tools the client has at the time of the trauma or if the client doesn't take the time to process emotional trauma with the tools they do have, these traumas take up residence in the physical body.

This isn't to punish the person. It's just temporary storage until the person has the tools and/or the time and energy to process and heal. Eventually, these traumas- and not all of them are of the Trauma with a capital "T" variety as some can be trauma with a little "t"- will resurface as physical pain or ailments when the person is ready to process them…OR when the storage facility is too full and cannot accept any more, which is an indication that it's time for the person to get some better tools and begin processing.

As Cynthia began to perform my client's emotional body scan, she once again got to the reproductive system and then shared some images with my client, letting her know what was stuck there. My client told me about being four years old, playing with a doll, and fantasizing about being a mother, specifically about being a better mother than the one she had.

She told the doll that she was going to love her always and forever, no matter what, and never punish her because she's just a baby and babies don't need punishment, they need love. She then went on to another memory of being in utero, not yet born. She said she felt scared because something had happened to make her mother afraid, and she immediately felt her mother's fear. I asked her to rise up out of the scene of this memory so she was no longer in her mother's womb and could understand what was happening.

"It was a car crash. Everyone survived, but I can see that my mother is pregnant and worrying about me. My father is there, but he seems angry more than scared. My mother is scared for me and also afraid of my father." I asked her to perceive this through the understanding of her Highest-Self, and she said, "He's actually not angry, but he doesn't know how to be scared without anger," and then my client's subconscious mind began speaking too, almost laughing. It then said, "Yes, that's it exactly! Every time I was afraid of him, it was me reacting to my mother reacting to his anger, which wasn't anger, but fear! I get it now." And then, "Oh, papa, I'm so sorry you never learned how to just be afraid. What a burden that must have been."

I asked if her papa was still alive, and she said, "No." I then asked if he was there with her now, and she said, "No," then, "Oh wait, YES! There he is. Hi papa! I love you and I understand you better now." I asked if he was available for a hug, and she said, "Yes, definitely. He is hugging me now. I can't hear him, but I think he's saying that he loves me too- but without words. I just know that's what he is saying." I asked if the soul of her miscarried baby was there too, and she said, "No. I don't see him anywhere," at which point she got a pain in her pelvis and began writhing around.

I was very glad I asked her to be in her bed for this session because had she just been in a chair, she would have likely writhed her way right out of it!

I asked if we could please go ahead and send some healing light and energy to her pelvis, and then she exclaimed, "It's HIM! He's still in me. Not his body but his…energy…or something. He never left. Oh, Jeremy, I see you now. You've been stuck in me this entire time." I asked if he was ready to let go and continue on with his soul's journey, and she went silent for several minutes before quietly crying. I felt it best to wait until she had experienced this precious moment before moving on. Eventually, she said, "He's ready, but I'm not. I don't want to let him go. I was supposed to be the best mother, and instead, I killed him. I was supposed to love him forever and always, no matter what, and it's me…I've kept him here. That's why I keep this extra weight on and why it's exactly the same as when he died. This is why I have pain, scar tissue, and guilt. So, so, so much guilt. And shame." She began crying louder and saying, "I'm so ashamed. I was supposed to give you the world, but instead, I killed you."

I asked her to let her highest self show her the reality of the situation and let her see all of this from the greater perspective, and she began nodding her head, and while still crying a little, she began to smile. She then said, "I understand now. There was something wrong with Jeremy's human heart, and it was not my fault. It's nobody's fault. He tried to repair it after he entered this body, but just couldn't, so he decided to leave and wait for a better opportunity." I asked, "When did he enter that little baby body in your womb?" She immediately, without any hesitation at all, said, "At 30 weeks."

I asked her highest consciousness if this was normal...if this was the usual time a soul entered into a human body, and it said, "Sometimes. Not always. It depends. Some know they need to help the mother or father or both sooner, so they enter earlier. Some wait until just before birth," I asked what is the soonest, and it said, "There is no soonest because the higher ones can orchestrate a baby, but they know the risks and accept them." So, of course, I had to ask, "Who are the 'Higher Ones?'" There was no response. I then asked, "What happens to babies that are aborted, since that's such a hot topic among us earth-bound folks?" It simply said, "There is no death. Only life. Some of you know this; others choose not to know. A fragment of the soul can get stuck or trapped if the mother vessel won't let go. So, part of them stays to...comfort...to help...but they lose track...they get lost...they forget... and those parts sometimes stay for a lifetime. Sometimes, many lifetimes. It's easy to forget."

This was all incredibly eye-opening to me because I, too, have experienced this type of loss. I was mind-blown at this point, but of course, I needed to stay present for my client, so I asked if it would be possible to release this soul fragment from my client so it could reunite with its own higher consciousness and continue its journey, letting my client also continue on hers. And this is where things got very, very interesting!

My client's Inner Healer, who had been silent through much of this, chimed in, "We need help. There is much damage to the energetic body." The energetic body, I have come to understand from sessions like this, is much bigger than the physical or emotional body and is essentially our antennae, amplifier, and receiver all in one. It is made up of waves and particles. It can effortlessly move from one of these states to the other, and it is affected by our emotions at any given time. It acts as both a magnet and a repellent and fluctuates between these states as well, all based on our emotions and expectations.

I asked the client to please invite all of her helpers and guides to help release this lost little soul fragment from her body, and she said that she felt as if everyone she's ever loved from this lifetime and beyond came to stand around her in a circle, and her father was there, beckoning to Jeremy to come to join in. He was reluctant at first because my client was still grieving and was not fully ready to let go. But as soon as she saw her father reach out and more or less scoop Jeremy's little soul fragment out of my client's womb, she sighed deeply, and her previously almost rigid body just went slack. It was the first time in our session I'd witnessed her completely surrender.

It's important to note here that complete relaxation is not necessarily indicative of a trance state when doing QJH. A person can be in a trance and not fully relaxed. It is preferable, but not necessary.

I asked my client's Inner Healer and highest consciousness if Jeremy was fully released, and I got a yes. I asked if we could go ahead and heal any damage done to my client's energetic, emotional, and physical bodies that were a result of this unintended attachment, and once again, I was told they needed more help. This was a first for me. WHO ELSE could possibly be required? And then my client said, "Wow. Okay. There is someone or something so vast that I can't see them. It's too bright. It's…I can't see anymore…but I can feel it. It's an angel. An archangel. It's Raphael. He is enveloping us all with his wings. It's so bright." She began crying again, but this time it was very obviously tears of joy as she was smiling bigger and bigger, and at one point, she just opened her eyes and said, "It is done."

I wasn't expecting that. I was taught to emerge hypnotic clients gently, not all at once like this, as it can result in a "hypnotic hangover". But in this session, she emerged all on her own with the sense of Archangel Raphael still healing her. She looked right at me, eyes wide open, and said, "It is done." What the…?

So, I asked if she was still in a trance, and she said, "No. I think for the first time ever, I see everything very clearly. It's like I've been UN-hypnotized or something!" We laughed at that, and I got her some water because her multidimensional consciousness just basically ran a marathon!

Fast forward to a year later, when I found out through social media that she'd given birth to a baby boy. I was amazed and incredibly curious as to why she hadn't even told me she was pregnant, especially because I sent out multiple follow-ups for every session. She responded that the whole experience was a little too crazy for her and that she honestly didn't even know where to start by telling me about it.

She said our session was all like a bizarre dream that she didn't understand, and she wasn't sure she even believed it. There was almost a sense of fear in her voice, so I told her, "I didn't heal anything. That was ALL you. I just facilitated the communication you needed in order to get what you were ready for. I couldn't take it away any more than I could gift you with this".

She seemed to feel better after that and sent me some photos of her very beautiful and healthy baby boy, to which I said, "Good job, mama," and she burst into happy tears.

A few months later, she emailed me that her religious upbringing didn't include some of the possibilities that she experienced in our session, so she concluded that I must have hypnotized her into having those experiences. She seemed to believe that I was so powerful that I bestowed this magical thing upon her and that, of course, meant that I could somehow also take it away. I assured her that this was not the case at all, but that it might be a cool superpower to have as long as I only used it for good.

"This is not uncommon in my field. People believe that the hypnotist has some sort of magical power. We don't, by the way. What

we have is the skill to take people into a state of consciousness where they can create changes.

There is another interesting thing that can, and often does, occur with hypnotic change-work called the Apex Problem. This is where the client makes changes within themselves so easily and effortlessly as a result of hypnosis that they honestly do not recall how they felt before the changes. As if the neural pathways themselves have shifted to such a degree that they no longer remember how they felt before the changes. Therefore, they don't have the ability to emotionally connect with how they felt before."

~Kryssa

Peace After a Loved One Passes

By Kryssa Marie Bowman

This client came to me because her husband had passed away three years prior to brain cancer, and he said some very cruel things to her shortly before his death as a result of the illness he was dying from and the combination of medications he was taking for that illness. Specifically, she said that her soul felt crushed.

Needless to say, these being his parting words to her hadn't set well, and she found herself questioning his love for her throughout their 40+ year marriage. She wanted a sense of closure and peace with her perception of him and their life together.

When we entered her Hallway of Answers in a trance state, I asked her which doorway revealed itself as the doorway she needed to explore to resolve these issues. She found it, and we went through it, at which point she found herself on a train heading west. She was surprised to discover that she was a man.

Her name was Aaron in that life, and Aaron's wife's name was Mary. They were heading west to start a new life, and as she fast-forwarded, she/he discovered they died unexpectedly of natural causes, leaving Mary to forge ahead with this new life with their young children, but without him. He was bereft. The consciousness that was my client said she realized that this was one of Aaron's exit points for that lifetime, but she didn't feel ready to leave now that it had happened. Her spirit, like Aaron, stuck around for a while to oversee Mary and their children before moving on to continue its soul's journey.

Then my client landed in a lifetime in the 1920s as a female and happily discovered that she was married to the same partner, though their genders were reversed. They owned and lived on an orchard, and her husband's name was Robert. They lived to a ripe old age and had many children together, one of whom she recognized as her sister in her current lifetime. She went through a brief and easy death in this lifetime and landed in another place. One that she struggled to put words to.

In this new place, she found many beings that she thought might be other souls, and they were happy and filled with light. These were not the lost souls she encountered while she/he was Aaron. I asked her to describe what she meant, and she said that when she chose to stick around for Mary and their children, he was in a darker, denser place that was populated with many lost souls, but he just ignored them because he was there for a purpose. His only focus then was on overseeing his wife and children.

But this new place was the place the soul went to when they finally let go and moved into the light. And it's where my client's soul went in between every lifetime. I asked how many lifetimes she's shared with her husband, including this lifetime, and she said, "Seven," without a moment's hesitation, and smiled.

There was no judgment in this new place, no sense of feeling sad at leaving the previous lifetimes, and there was a greater vantage point where one could glimpse into these human lives without feeling emotionally bound to them, she explained. She felt very peaceful, loved, and supported, but she was not yet welcomed, as it wasn't her time to join them.

I then invited the soul that was her husband in this life to please visit with her so she could gain the closure she was requesting, and he showed up on something like a cosmic surfboard!

He said that he was so sorry for the last words he said to her and blamed it on faulty machinery. He said it was the diseased brain in that body that was speaking and not his soul. The consciousness of his body and brain was temporary and not the same consciousness as his soul. His soul loved her.

It said she was his "favorite" and that he'd been surfing the universe while waiting for her to join him. I asked if there were any other doors we needed to explore, any other lifetimes or souls that she needed to visit, and she said, "No, we are in alignment now," and then, "Thank you".

I emerged my client gently and she just sat there for a good 10 minutes in near silence, with tears of joy streaming down her face, and when she got up to leave, she was no longer walking hunched over or with the slight limp she had when she first arrived. We hadn't done any specific healing work on her body, so we were both a little surprised, but she said she felt "lighter" than she could ever remember feeling.

A week later, this client sent me a text message saying, "I still feel connected to my husband, but in a light and joyful way. You have no idea how this has changed my entire life!"

I don't have the right to speak on the validity of this phenomenal experience for my client or offer up my personal beliefs. All I can say is that she came to me with a request to resolve her pain, and I helped her find the parts of her that could do exactly that. Did she actually communicate with the spirit of her departed husband? Maybe.

Did she receive the resolution she was seeking? Definitely.

Did she feel better about her marriage and her life as a result of this Quantum Journeys session? Absolutely.

Would it have been helpful for me to point out to her that there's scant scientific evidence that what she experienced was objectively and measurably "real"?

I don't think so. Do you?

The one thing I stand firm on in my sessions, and what I teach QJH my students, is to let our clients have their own unique experiences in a space of acceptance and support.

~Kryssa

Are Ghosts Just Fragments That Get Left Behind?

By Kryssa Marie Bowman

This client was a teenage girl who spontaneously went into a past life when I asked her Highest-Self to guide us to wherever she needed to go in order to clear up some intrusive anxiety she'd been experiencing.

Kryssa: Now that we're through the doorway, take a moment to adjust and tell me whatever it is that you're seeing, sensing, or experiencing.

Client: I'm at a farm.

K: Tell me about this farm.

C: Nobody is here.

K: What kind of farm is it? Are there animals?

C: Yes, but they're quiet. There's a house.

K: What does the house look like?

C: White. Old.

K: Is it old now, or does it seem like an old style?

C: Both.

K: Tell me more.

C: It's very gloomy. It feels almost heavy.

K: Where is everyone?

C: I don't know.

K: Do you get the sense that they're in the house?

C: Sort of.

K: What is the sense of the gloominess about? And before we explore any further, let's ask your highest consciousness to share with you why it feels gloomy.

C: I'm scared.

K: Look down at your shoes and tell me what kind of shoes you're wearing.

C: I'm a kid.

K: How old are you?

C: Five.

K: And what are you afraid of?

C: The sky.

K: What does the sky look like?

C: There's a storm.

K: I'm going to ask you some questions and just allow your highest consciousness to drop the answers into your awareness. Where are you? Just let it come.

C: I think there's a tornado.

K: What year is it?

C: 19-something.

K: Where are you?

C: I'm in the U.S....the middle. It's very flat.

K: 19 what? Just think back to a conversation you heard, maybe your parents...

C: 1984.

K: And what is your name?

C: Claire.

K: And Claire, what happened in this lifetime in 1984 in the U.S. with this tornado? Just allow the answers to come easily.

C: I can't get back inside.

K: Where is everybody else?

C: They're in the living room.

K: Do they know you're missing?

C: Yes. But they're not coming to look for me. I feel lost. Why aren't they coming to get me?

K: Fast forward a bit and tell me what else happens, but let's have you watch what's happening from the outside instead of inside Claire.

C: She's crying. She knows she died.

K: Does she see the light?

C: No.

K: What does she decide to do?

C: She's just standing there in the living room.

K: So she goes to be with her family?

C: Yes. They are also scared.

K: Let's fast forward a bit more. Does Claire see the light?

C: Yes. She doesn't want to go to it. She wants to stay with her family.

K: Let's check in and see where she is now. Just reach out and say, "Claire, where are you now?" and find out whatever we find out.

C: She's still there at the farmhouse.

K: Is there anyone there with her?

C: No. There's nobody.

K: Would she like to now go ahead and continue on her journey and be reunited with them?

C: Yes.

K: Would you like to help her?

C: Yes.

K: Let's go and have you meet her. Does she recognize you?

C: Yes.

K: Beautiful. You can now find that portal of light where she can reunite with her loved ones and not be so alone anymore. Do you see it?

C: Yes, it's in the upper right corner.

K: Perfect. Let's remind her right now that she can go now. You can hold her hand so she's not scared. And it may feel familiar to you.

C: She's still scared.

K: It's ok. You've got her now. Once she moves into it, she can reunite with her family, and we can ask that she reintegrate with her soul. Just hold her hand, and as soon as she gets through, she's going to be so happy to be with her loved ones again. Does this help her not be so afraid?

C: Yes. She feels better. She feels safe now.

K: Yes! Let's invite her ancestors and guides to greet her and surround her with love, protect her, and take her into their arms to let her move into this next phase of her journey. Who shows up?

C: Her mom.

K: Is her mom incarnated now, or did she move on too?

C: I don't know. She's with my grandma now. They're hugging each other. She's happy now.

K: I would like to ask your highest consciousness how this has impacted you now, in this incarnation.

C: She's not so scared. I'm not so scared anymore.

K: Perfect. Let's please also call back any fragments that have been left behind, call back any power and energy that was stuck there or elsewhere, and allow them to reintegrate with the soul that you, too, are a part of. Let's just go ahead and do a full system reset as we bring light into the spaces where any damage has been done, finding any blockages or injuries or ailments on all levels, layers, densities, and dimensions, and let them soften and begin to flow- releasing whatever needs to be released. Just letting go of any unnecessary trauma. Anything that no longer needs to be carried, let go of it for your ultimate highest good. And speaking now to your highest consciousness, can you please let her know how absolutely loved and loveable and cared for and protected she truly is in the grand scheme of all that is?

C: She's sharing it silently. I feel it.

Prior to this session, it hadn't occurred to me that a soul could be fractalized to the degree that some fractals could get stuck elsewhere and not return to their source. I guess I just assumed that when our physical bodies die, we return to our higher consciousness, or soul. So, this particular session was very eye-opening for me. The concept that parts of our consciousness can get stuck in a place that is adjacent to the 3D world was new, and yet it makes sense as far as the concept of ghosts is concerned.

The part of our consciousness having these incarnated 3D experiences wants to make sense of it all...but perhaps the rest of our consciousness designed it so that we simply can't. Not here anyway. The best we can do is be open to all of the various possibilities and not ascribe any particular belief system to them.

~Kryssa

A Past Life Brings Joy and Safety to a Current Life

By Kryssa Marie Bowman

Since I do my best not to lead my clients to any particular place while in hypnosis, their consciousness is given free rein to explore whatever comes up for them while in a trance state. My job then is simply to support their experience, even if- or when- it's not at all what I'm expecting.

We often start with a hallway with many doors, and I ask only that they allow their own higher consciousness to point out which doorway they most need to explore. Sometimes, my clients find what they need right there in the hallway! This particular client found herself drawn to a fireplace with a library that was at the end of a long, dark wooden hallway.

When she got there, there was a particular book that just found its way onto her lap as she sat in this reclining chair by the fire. Experience has taught me not to derail this. When a book shows up, it MUST be paid attention to!

She opened the book and saw the acknowledgments, but she couldn't make them out. She felt compelled to turn to the next page, and there was just a little pencil drawing. This pencil drawing began to come to life, and it was a little girl. She was in this quaint but very old European village with a cobblestone street, and there was a donkey and a flower cart.

I asked if it was in her highest good to check it out, and suddenly, she found herself inside the drawing.

I suggested that she go ahead and open her mind's eye to whatever this picture was about and allow all of the colors to come to life. Just dial all of her senses wide open so that she could see and feel and smell and touch and taste this environment.

When she got fully immersed in her various senses, I asked her to look down and tell me what she was wearing on her feet.

She said she had a little black Mary Janes.

I said, "Ok, what else are you wearing?"

She said, "It looks like I have on little socks and a dress with an apron, kind of like Alice in Wonderland."

"Ok, how old are you?" I asked, and she said, "I think I'm five."

I then asked, "What's your name?"

"Elsa," she then proceeded to tell me about this lifetime that she had as a little girl named Elsa. She lived in France a long time ago, and she was very happy and contented and fulfilled and not afraid and had no anxiety whatsoever.

When I asked her highest consciousness to explain why it brought us to this lifetime, because you see, her desire was to dig deep into her past to understand why she's been having so much anxiety, and it said, "Just wait and see".

Her highest consciousness then explained that it wasn't necessary to go find out why; it was only necessary that she remember how to live without fear and pain.

Then a little kitten named Daisy arrived on the scene-Elsa's kitten from that lifetime- which helped her anchor in the joy and safety she felt then. She came back out of the book and into the little area with the fireplace and the library, and it wasn't necessary to go find anything else.

Her highest consciousness then said, "It was done. She's got it now. She doesn't need to go excavating all of the reasons why she's been struggling. She just needed to get out of the old pattern of expecting pain and recall that she had other programs she could call upon instead."

Interestingly, after the session, she told me that she was a dog person, but that she's been caring for a cat that initially belonged to her daughter for the past few months.

What a beautiful session.

This particular client requested help with releasing negative thoughts and emotions that she believed were the result of unhealed trauma. Her Higher-Self took her to a past life memory full of love and joy instead of digging through her childhood to address painful memories. This is a perfect example of how QJH is different from other forms of hypnotherapy. If I had been in the driver's seat, I may have inadvertently taken her to places in her past that she was not yet ready to address. But by putting her Higher-Self in the driver's seat, it knew that what she most needed was to recall what it feels like to be happy, fulfilled, grateful, and loved, not to dredge up old pain. Not everyone is capable of revisiting ancient trauma and coming out unscathed. And no matter how careful the hypnotist may be to avoid retraumatization, it can still happen. I've both witnessed this as well as experienced it myself when I was studying regression-to-cause hypnosis. But the client's Highest-Self always knows exactly what they need and how to deliver it.

~Kryssa

End of Atlantis

By Kryssa Marie Bowman

This client came to me due to what she termed a "dysregulated nervous system". She was experiencing fight or flight responses regularly, and they were disrupting her day-to-day life, as well as her ability to sleep. I approached this session with the intention of simply helping her release this anxiety and providing her with some helpful tools to manage it when it comes up unnecessarily. I say unnecessarily because it's not only impossible to completely eliminate anxiety, but it's also not helpful to do so.

Our brains and nervous systems are designed to experience anxiety as a warning signal when there is a threat to our survival. However, our brains and nervous systems can get stuck in a loop of anxiety when there's no resolution to the threat, and/or it gets retriggered by any number of variables. These variables can be as simple as an anniversary of a traumatic event, or a reminder in the form of a person, place, smell, sound, etc. So, I see my job as that of helping my clients identify what needs resolving, seeking that resolution, then releasing the mechanism running that program and installing tools to either counter-balance it or get a system reset.

When the trauma occurs in the current lifetime, this can be a relatively simple process. Sometimes, regression to the trauma and assessing it from a different perspective is helpful. Other times, it might be best to skirt the original trauma and come at it from the level of the beliefs that were installed due to the trauma and deal with those beliefs directly. Sometimes it's just an accidental habit the subconscious mind picked up to help the person feel safe, when in fact, it's causing them to feel an underlying level of fear that results in hypervigilance- as in the case of PTSD- and it's more helpful to neutralize the trauma at the level of the neural pathways involved in the habit of fear and provide the means to access more resourceful neural pathways.

However, in my work, I've found that some traumas don't originate in this lifetime. I call these Shadow Traumas. I have no way of knowing if this is the case unless the client comes to me with this knowledge in advance, perhaps from some other past life regression or from dreams or visions received in meditation. But even then, I don't change my approach. I don't assume that we're dealing with past or other life trauma, even if the client is positive that's the case. In fact, I've found it best not to assume anything, ever. I simply take them into a trance state and ASK.

So, in this client's case, when we set about asking her higher consciousness to reveal the doorway where she could get the help she needed, she found herself going through a doorway that led to a place where it was "cool and breezy". I asked her to look down at her feet, as that is often a helpful way for the client to get a better understanding of where (or when) they are, and she said she had on "scuba diving fins" and she could see a "wall of water" on the horizon.

I asked where she was, and she said, "Atlantis," and that she was at the end of this particular lifetime.

I asked her to rewind a little bit, to go back to before the wall of water, and as she did, her name in that lifetime came to her. She wasn't sure if it was her name or her job, but the name "Forester" came to her, and she realized that she was a man. She said he worked for the government and that he was aware that everyone was going to die soon. She realised that Forester "was a pawn in the war" and she was acting on orders from above. That her job was to destroy this civilization, but she didn't want to. I asked her why this civilization needed to be destroyed, and she said, "It's not clear. You're not supposed to ask questions. You're just supposed to take orders."

I asked her to find the part of her consciousness that does know why. Once again, I said, "Why was this civilization destroyed? What was the purpose?"

Client: There was a war."

Kryssa: A war between who?

C: Between this world and the other world.

K: Who are the beings of the other world?

C: They're scaly and green. They look kind of like Gremlin's from that Gremlin movie. Reptilian. They are about 6 feet tall. Humans are only 5 feet tall. The humans have been around for 6 billion years.

K: Have humans always been on Earth for these 6 billion years?

C: No.

K: Where else have humans been?

C: Other planets. Outside of the Milky Way, there are other human consciousnesses.

K: Are we still at war?

C: Yes

K: Where are we at with that war?

C: We're in the eye of it.

K: Are we winning?

C: Not at this time?

K: Is there hope for humans?

C: There is hope, but…., and she trailed off with tears in her eyes.

K: What do we need to do?

C: We have to walk through the fear. Let go of the fear that we don't know everything. Be at peace that we can't know everything. To just trust.

K: Does this have anything to do with the fear that [client's name] is currently experiencing?

The client then switched to the voice of an aspect of her higher consciousness.

C: Yes. She's a very perceptive human, and she feels dark energy. She feels it among certain people, and it sticks to her almost…like tar.

K: What can we do to help her in this life? Can we help her to observe it but not absorb it?

C: Yes, but there's this one person in her life that has reptilian energy, and she feels drawn to it.

K: Can we protect her from this?"

C: Yes. I'm bringing in more divine resources from the top of her head. She is drawn to this dark energy because she believes she failed humanity in Atlantis. She is trying to resolve it. It's not necessary, though.

K: Can you talk more about why it's no longer necessary?

C: Karma. She, like so many others, got stuck in the belief of karmic balancing. But there really is no such thing. The idea of karma comes from darkness, not light. It is how they keep us stuck in this cycle.

K: Can you help [client's name] step out of the cycle of karma? Can you help liberate her from this belief?

C: I have been trying. She has been indoctrinated through guilt and shame, and this makes it difficult for her to experience the light. She believes she needs to be punished; therefore, she is punished.

K: How many lifetimes has she experienced due to this belief in karma?

C: MANY! I think she is nearing the end, though. This is why we arranged for her to meet you.

K: Me? Why me?

C: Because you have stepped out many times before, and you come back to help others. We thank you for this.

K: Please tell me how I can best assist her.

C: Keep showing her the light. Help her become open to receiving it. We cannot force this. It must be a collaboration.

K: Can I do this even though I, myself, struggle to remain in the light?

C: Yes. This is your path. You chose to be a conduit of light...which means you must recognize the light being hidden by darkness. You cannot do that without also being aware of the dark. Sometimes, you feel consumed by it until you find your way out, so you can help others find their way out.

K: I have goosebumps all over when you say that. Yet, right here and right now, I have a human client who has hired me to help her no longer have chronic anxiety. What can we do right to make her current experience more comfortable?

C: You are already doing it. We will help. Ultimately, she has to choose to release herself from the illusion of karmic balancing. You are not the first to help her with this. The programs of shame and guilt run deep in your species.

K: Can you explain this programming?

C: It was a program installed to help you evolve more rapidly. It was intended to yield compassion, but it was usurped by the Anu to make you more obedient and pliable to their will. Compassion is a high state of being. High-frequency states of being are not controllable.

K: Ah, yes. That makes sense. So, who usurped this?

C: The reptilians.

K: Can you explain why?

C: We already have. Now it is time to let go of the need to understand everything and trust that by surrendering to the light, we will be there to help. Physical lives come and go. That is the nature of choosing a physical incarnation. To fully experience thoughts and beliefs in that dimension as they unfold, but it is not necessary to hold onto them, to repeat them for the sake of karmic balance. Experience them if you choose, but ultimately, you must let them go.

K: You do realise that when we come into these 3D human lives, everything feels very intense and real and impossible to just release without some sort of balance or resolution, don't you?

C: Yes. That is the current programming. This is changing. As more of you wake up to your true essence, you will discover that karma is self-imposed.

K: Self-imposed or programmed by reptilians?

C: Ha! Yes. Now you understand. The term you use is 'drinking the Kool-Aid'.

K: Haha, yes. Thank you. Getting back to how to help [client's name] with her current issues of anxiety and sleeplessness, what can we do to help her?

C: We will fill her with light. She needs to get outside and drink more water. Start her day with a meditative practice so we can communicate with her.

K: Do you have any other specific advice for her? Are you able to see or feel the aspects of her subconscious mind and body that need help?

C: She needs to have the stuck energy massaged in her belly. To let it soften and flow again. She needs to meditate on bringing the pieces of her that have been left behind, or have been taken, or are broken and fractured beyond.

K: Can we just do that NOW? Right here, call back any and all fractals that she has given up or been taken from her throughout her lifetimes, levels, densities, and dimensions, and reintegrate them if that's in her highest good.

C: Yes. We are doing that now. There is an icicle lodged in her belly that she is ready to release now.

K: Thank you for helping her to release that now. I am so honored to work with you. Do you have a name I can honor you with after all of this work together?

C: Borealis.

K: It's an honor to make your acquaintance, Borealis, and I thank you for all of your help. Do you know that this word already exists in human language?

C: Yes. We chose this name. It is in your language because we gifted it to you. We are of the light. Many spectrums.

K: Is there anything else that needs to be addressed for this human named [client's name]?

C: Yes. She needs to see her soul arc. She is here on purpose. She has a purpose. She chose this, and she is powerful beyond her current understanding. She needs to trust that her path is exactly what she chose and that she can help so many others by accepting it and finding the gold in it.

K: The gold?

C: The golden. Golden light. It's no longer necessary for her to play in the dark. She is on the precipice of evolving and only needs to make the choice to step into the light that is already there.

K: I will remind her of this. Thank you.

I gently brought her out of her trance at this point and offered some post-hypnotic suggestions that she "would feel wonderful...resolved, revitalized, rejuvenated, reactivated and reset".

And here is where I would love to tell you that her QJH experience was nothing short of wonderful, amazing, and life-changing, but the truth is that she ended up cancelling all of our future sessions.

She was scheduled to have two more.

I was at a loss to explain to myself why she no longer wanted to explore her multidimensional consciousness, as it was one of the most phenomenal sessions I'd ever experienced! But I realised that this was my own ego demanding recognition.

And you know what? IT'S NOT ABOUT ME!

She got what she needed from that session because it was her highest consciousness that tapped into the collective of humanity- and it's not for me to validate or invalidate her experience or how she integrated it after the fact. I will always be humbled by and thankful for this conversation with "Borealis", whoever and whatever that is.

When my clients say things that seem impossible, like "humans have been here for 6 billion years", I don't ever invalidate or discount them. This is their experience, and it's not for me to interpret or correct. Who knows whether there's truth to this or not? There is mounting evidence suggesting that humans have been around much longer than previously thought, and speculation that there may have even been multiple human civilizations that rose and fell prior to our current one. For the purposes of this session, it doesn't matter. What matters is my client's interpretation of these memories and experiences, and most importantly, how she integrated whatever she needed to integrate and released whatever she needed to release. It's not up to me what she integrates or releases, because I can't possibly know what she needs more than her own Higher-Self knows, which is why my job is to ask questions. Facilitate conversations. Help my clients help themselves rather than take on the role of being their healer. They are their own healer. Always.

This was one of the first sessions I had with someone who recalled a past life during the fall of Atlantis. I've had several since then. In one of them, I thought to ask my client's higher consciousness if there was any particular reason I was having so many sessions with people who recalled being present at the fall of Atlantis. I was told that many have returned and are returning now in order to save the human race from experiencing an even more catastrophic fall than the Atlantean one. That we are, once again, in a battle for our autonomy and evolution of consciousness, and that by saving us this time, they will be able to release the guilt they've been carrying around as a shadow trauma throughout these many lifetimes. That they are here to balance the scales, so to speak.

~Kryssa

When You Don't Know That You Know

By Kryssa Marie Bowman

I had a session today with a woman who has already had two successful sessions with me on gracefully moving the grief of several departed loved ones. She had some remarkable experiences involving her loved ones and other guides and helpers in our first two sessions.

Today, she wanted to experience some other lifetimes and possibly explore the life between lives (author and hypnotherapist Michael Newton's term for past life regression that regresses to in between incarnations), so she could get a sense of how no one really dies. She was 76 and had almost no family left, so death had been on her mind more and more lately.

She got all of that and so much more!

However, after almost every question I asked, before she even gave herself the opportunity to let the answer come, she would immediately and almost compulsively say, "I don't know,"…to which I would have to find various ways of saying, "What if you did know?" and then the answer would be right there.

She was hopping easily from lifetime to lifetime, but the part of her subconscious mind that was taught not to trust herself, that was dismissed and invalidated and disbelieved by her husband and earlier by her birth family, just refused to give up.

We'd already addressed several other parts that were getting in the way of resource/ego state transformation, but this one was relentless and, in the end, unsuccessful.

Because she DID know, and in the last 10 minutes, she finally stopped responding with "I don't know," and just let the information flow. Things moved very rapidly from there!

I'm sharing this because sometimes, no matter what you, the hypnotist, say or do, the client just needs to come to some sort of internal agreement that you may not even be aware of.

So, it's important to allow time and space for that.

She went to France in 1863, then to ancient Rome and Egypt. She's had 12 Earth Lifetimes and a revolving cast of the same characters in different roles. Her higher consciousness deemed it not in her highest good to reveal any non-Earth-based lifetimes, but it did say that she had some.

When she finally stopped jumping through lifetimes, which was what her own higher consciousness was choosing to do and had nothing to do with me intentionally taking her to them, I asked, "How have these brief visits to various lifetimes helped you?" She was quiet for a moment and then said, "I feel comforted in knowing that when we die, we don't really die. I'm not afraid of death, but I am afraid of never seeing my son or my husband or my father again. But I saw all of them in those lifetimes! They were different versions of themselves, but I recognized them, and I'm so happy to know that I'll be reunited with them again someday soon".

Then her son's energy came through and told her he loved her, and that he is happy and he watches over her regularly. She said she could feel him when he was with her. He gave her a big hug, and as he did so, I watched her whole body relax even more, and her face became filled with joy. Tears came to her eyes, and she said she felt as if he'd reached in and filled her heart with pure love.

Then her husband came to say hi, and she couldn't hear what he was saying for some reason, so I asked her higher consciousness if we could adjust the frequency in order to hear him better. It said yes, and then she was able to make out that he was telling her

"Everything is going to be ok" and that he was "waiting for her on the other side" whenever she's ready to join him. "But not too soon" because she "still has more love to give" in this lifetime. She nodded her head and seemed to understand.

And then a new visitor came, and she said he was so big that she couldn't see the whole of him. She felt certain it was a man, but he was so bright and full of white light and really tall, and then she saw he had wings. I asked her to ask him what he calls himself, and she said "Archangel Michael".

She said he had a message for her, but it was only for her, and so she asked if it was okay not to share it with me. I chuckled and said, this is your session, and I have no authority over archangels, so you can do and say, or not do and say, whatever you like. I asked her to just let me know when she was ready to move on. She smiled then and opened her eyes, though clearly still in a trance, and she said "Thank you" to something she was apparently seeing right in front of her. Then she closed her eyes again and said, "I'm ready".

I asked if there was anything else we needed to explore or address for her highest good today, and her Higher-Self said we were done. I asked if it had any other advice or suggestions or praise to offer, and it said, "She knows who she is now, and how very loved she is, so all is done".

I gently emerged her and when she came all the way back, I asked her how she felt She said she felt a level of peace she didn't recall ever feeling before and that she was just so tickled to reunite with some of her lost loved ones. Then she laughed and said, "I guess they're not lost anymore". I laughed also and said, "I'm so glad that you gave yourself permission to trust what you were experiencing. I wasn't sure if we were going to break through the I-don't-knows. Then she smiled and said, "Yeah. That's an old and not very good habit of mine. But I know now. And I know that I know, so I think that habit may be over now".

> *I absolutely love it when clients have archangel visitations.   I wasn't raised with any particular religion, and so prior to these visitations within my sessions, my knowledge and understanding of archangels was very limited.   I thought they were specific to the Catholic church. And it was actually Archangel Michael that corrected me on that point, and not in a whimsical manner either!*

He, of all the archangels that have visited in my sessions, is the most serious. He's actually rather intimidating sometimes, and I learned quickly not to try to joke around with him.

The first time Archangel Michael showed up in a session, I asked my client if they were raised Catholic. They said no, and then Michael himself channeled through my client and in a rather stern and booming voice said, "I have no religion. I am here for all humans!". I sheepishly said, "My mistake and my apologies for now knowing more about you. Thank you for clearing that up for me.

~Kryssa

Binge Eating Origins

By Kryssa Marie Bowman

I facilitated a session today for a woman with a binge eating disorder. It was her second session, and we'd already visited with her Inner Healer. In the first session, she received so much healing and felt much better about herself, and was already eating healthier and in ideal quantities…but she was still struggling with one aspect-- sweets. So, this time, I just had her go to the Hallway of Answers and ask for her Highest-Self to reveal which doorway we needed to go through in order to resolve this issue of not being able to say no to sweets. This essentially made her own intuition guide her without any specific guidance from me.

The doorway that was revealed led her to a childhood scene where she essentially regressed to the cause of her issue.

The scene that she entered had to do with being punished for wanting a second piece of cake when she was six years old. The punishment was that she was forced to eat the rest of the cake while her mother made pig sounds at her. It's important to note that she was witnessing this as an objective observer rather than as her childhood self. She then noticed another doorway and felt drawn to it with curiosity. I suggested we check it out because anything being revealed here was worthy of exploration.

She went through and found another scene where she was a little younger and at a relative's birthday party with her mother. She asked for a second piece of cake in this scene as well, and her mother snapped at her, this time humiliating her in front of all the guests and family. She was absolutely mortified and embarrassed and wanted to disappear. This would be considered a "sensitizing event," and the previous scene would be considered an "activating event" in the jargon of professional hypno folks.

So, I dusted off my regression tools and we went and rescued that little girl. I suggested that the adult version tell the child version all the things she needed to hear in those moments. She told her how sweet and wonderful and full of love and curiosity she was, and that it was perfectly normal and natural to want more of the cake. That there is no inherent shame in wanting or even eating cake. Then she dialogued with her mother, allowing her mother to apologize for not realizing the damage she had caused and to explain that she herself was raised to believe girls and women had to be thin in order to be valuable in our society.

That she, the mother, had spent her entire life focused on maintaining a thin body at all costs, denying herself constantly as she dieted from the age of 11 years old until the day she died, and that she deeply regrets wasting so much of her life on this. That she regrets even more the harm this caused her beloved daughter. The spirit mother then gave her a hug and told her she didn't want her carrying this ugly baggage even one step further, and asked her daughter to please give it back. To release it and give it back, so this mother could give it back to her own mother, and so on, until they found its origins and then heal it at its source.

She visualized it in the form of actual baggage, like an old turn-of-the-century piece of luggage, and it kept being passed back generation after generation until it found its original owner, and it was a great-great-great-great-grandfather. He accepted it with deep shame and proceeded to open it up and release each aspect of it that had accumulated through the centuries. When it was empty, he burned it. My client just watched all of this in pure fascination, barely audible as she described what she was experiencing.

Then, some Spirit Guides showed up and joined all of these ancestors, and together, they surrounded my client with love and support. The scene itself disappeared, and she found herself in a massive white room that could barely contain the multitude of helpers and supporters that had come to help. My client began crying tears of joy and said that she could feel the healing of her family through her own heart. She expressed that she had never felt so much love, so much support, or so much light ever before.

What I really appreciated was that it was HER OWN intuition that led her there, rather than me intentionally taking her to painful childhood memories. This, in my opinion, is the ONLY way to conduct hypnotic regression. If a scene comes up organically, naturally, without any leading at all, then this means that the client is absolutely ready to explore them and heal from them. Forcing a person to explore old traumas that their subconscious intentionally repressed runs the risk of retraumatizing the client.

*For the hypno pros: That could have also just as easily turned into a more traditional timeline session or even a parts therapy/ego-resource states session. But that's one of the things I love about Quantum

Journeys Hypnosis…the adaptability and room for creatively bringing together all sorts of tools.

If you're at all familiar with my work, you have probably heard me warn colleagues of the inherent risks involved in regression-to-cause hypnosis techniques. I'm not the only one. It actually fell out of favor in the 1990s after a rash of patients reported what turned out to be false memory implantations throughout the 1980s. Implanting false memories has the same effects as recalling actual traumatic memories.

Our brains cannot tell the difference between imaginary and real. We know this to be true based on CAT scans of humans pretending to play piano and actually playing piano…the exact same areas of the brain register the exact same levels of activity.

The other risk is accidental retraumatization by having a client recall a repressed memory before they are ready to or have the tools to handle it. And it's not always obvious IN the session, as the effects of retraumatization show up weeks or even months later, after that particular memory reawakens the previously repressed neural pathways involved, and over time, the retriggered neural pathway begins to wreak the same kinds of havoc initially associated with the original traumatic event.

So, because of this, I very rarely intentionally use regression-to-cause, and when I do, I have several measures in place designed to prevent retraumatization. One of these is to allow the client's Highest-Self- the part that loves them always and only ever wants the best for them- to lead the session rather than have me lead it. Let them naturally and gently rediscover the necessary memories rather than me intentionally digging around their most wounded and vulnerable aspects.

My philosophy on this is that if the client's Highest-Self guides them to naturally and easily enter into a previously repressed memory, rather than me forcing it, then we're successfully avoiding both of the above-mentioned risks. I also make sure that we take the time to rewire the reawakened neural pathway by directing it to a positive place rather than just leaving it retriggered, vulnerable, and raw like a spliced-off electrical cord with full current running through it.

And as I said, I rarely use regression-to-cause, but there are some issues where it is extremely helpful. Disordered eating and negative body image issues are two that can deeply benefit from exploring the origins. This was my original niche, and I still specialize in it because I myself had anorexia as an adolescent. This morphed into bulimia in my later teen years and early 20s, and then orthoexia, which is where healthy eating becomes its own obsession and addiction, in the 30s. Overcoming disordered eating required me to heal my negative body image issues, but it took me decades because I didn't have a hypnotherapist to help me. I went the traditional counseling route, and they don't tackle both of these issues simultaneously, so it's easy to backslide or not make much progress. Because of this, I am still very passionate about helping others overcome their own disordered eating and harmful body image issues.

~Kryssa

Professional Hypnotist Who Thought She Couldn't Be Hypnotized

By Leslee Edmonson

One of my practice clients is a close friend who is a certified hypnotist, but has never done anything with it. She told me that no one has ever been able to hypnotize her and that during her practice sessions as a student, she simply couldn't experience what she was being asked to experience.

We did some ego/resource state transformation and then visited her Happy Safe Place. I noticed that her verbalization of the experience lacked a lot of visual and auditory descriptions, but included things like "a sense of surrender" and knowing that she was safe.

When we ascended to the hallway, she paused for a long time and said, "I can't seem to find it." So, I asked her if she could sense the expansiveness of a hallway in front of her and the possibilities and potential opportunities that were waiting behind its many doorways. I told her that she may simply know that she had arrived before she saw anything. Suddenly, she knew she had arrived and described a beautiful crystal hallway with raw crystals growing out of every door - she said she could sense their energetic qualities coming from each door. I continued to use the words "sense" and "know" throughout the remainder of the session, and it went very well.

Afterward, she expressed how blown away she was by the vividness of her experience. I then told her Kryssa's story about being more cognitive and getting pulled out of a trance when someone would tell her to see or hear something. That's when Kristin exclaimed, "Oh my goodness, that's me!" She said that she would tell herself hypnosis wasn't working, that she wasn't capable of being hypnotized, and suddenly, her lovely trance state would be replaced by a sense of failure and frustration.

Thank you, Kryssa, for helping me understand that everyone experiences hypnosis differently and for paying close attention to the cues my clients are giving me. Kristin and I had a great session together, and she wants to work together again soon so she can once again experience this profound state of trance.

We all have different senses that are stronger than others. Most hypnosis schools tend to focus on teaching inductions and styles of hypnotherapy that rely heavily on the visual sense. But not everyone has a strong visual imagination…myself included. People with no ability to visualize are considered to have Aphantasia, something I am learning more and more about as a result of my association with Paulina Trevena. For example, I've learned that aphantasia exists on a spectrum and some people are sensory blind across the board- without the ability to imagine seeing, hearing, smelling, feeling, etc. Others are only low in one area, often visual, and when within that, there are some who can imagine the outline of a thing, or the shape, but not full, graphic details.

Or, there are people like me who don't visualize very well but can cognitively imagine what a thing would feel like if we could see it, which works just as well for many of us.

There is also synesthesia, which is when two or more senses are connected, like the ability to see sound or smell words. This fascinates me, and I have tried to intentionally bring myself the synesthetic ability to see sound using self-hypnosis, but given that I'm not a strong visualizer to begin with, it's been slow going.

There are many theories as to why some people can and some can't visualize, and some are in between. Some say it's just how the brain is wired...perhaps a genetic blueprint. Some say it's the result of trauma. As with pretty much all things, I don't tend to believe there's a one-size-fits-all solution to this. In my own case, I remember being able to visualize very well as a child. Too well, perhaps, as I later got bullied for having an imaginary friend. Which might explain why my subconscious perhaps stepped in and intentionally turned the volume way down on that particular sense. To dull it to the degree that it saved me from being bullied anymore.

All these years later, and I've had some success in turning the volume back up again while in trance states. It's still not consistent, but I'm getting much better! Hypnosis is a fantastic tool for developing any/all of our senses IF we're physiologically capable. QJH has helped numerous people, clients, and students alike develop extrasensory perceptions as well.

~Kryssa

Healing the Inner Child Through Higher-Self

By Carolyn Mather

The client wanted to develop her business, release the need to know everything and overthink everything before taking action, release blockages and judgements around being able to sell herself and showcase her work, as she has always been told it is bad to 'brag'. She also wanted to release the idea that abundance has to come from a man or that she needs others to validate her value. She wanted to acquire the ability to showcase her work to others and let herself shine, understand how to do this in a way that is motivating and enjoyable, and transform so that she is able to showcase her work, put herself out there, talk to people about what she does, gain clients, and make a living from her business.

We met with the client's higher-self and asked for help with these goals, which it agreed to. The higher-self healed 'rigidity' and stiffness from parts of the client's body and explained that the rigidity was preventing them from achieving their aims. The higher-self told us that the blockages were linked to the client's mother and went back through many generations- it was 'ancestral' energy and a pattern, and it was traced all the way back through multiple generations, to the earliest one- a little girl who was in chains.

The higher-self then showed the little girl compassion and love, and also showed her different things that women are able to do now that they wouldn't have been able to back then- showing her that women are now able to dress how they want, go on nights out, drink alcohol, and own their own homes. The little girl was amazed by this. The shackles were then released from the little girl, and she began to shine brightly. The little girl then healed all the issues all the way down throughout the other generations. The client's higher-self put the light back into the client and let her know that she needed to shine from within.

The Higher-Self also gave her a practice to do daily to help her shine and told her she needed to practice heart breathing. The higher-self helped the client to see that when she was sharing the work she does, she is sharing love with others, and she came up with the phrase to represent this- 'there's a love party and you are invited'. The client's higher-self also showed the client in a sort of cave, chipping away at rocks, which she described as carving out her place in the marketplace.

The higher-self told the client that, as well as chipping away at the rock, she could also work with a Play-Doh-like material that is more malleable- showing her there are different ways she can work at things, not just one method. The client was told by her higher-self that she needed to have regular meetings with the spirit and energy of her business and needed to see these as things that are set commitments that need to be honored, and gave advice on where best to hold these meetings.

The higher-self showed her that developing her business is a flow between herself and the business and that instead of it just being her energy getting depleted by working on the business, it is like a 2-way flow, like an 'infinity' symbol, and the client gained the insight that because it is more of collaborative energy between them and the business, they won't always be able to control everything. The higher-self told the client she could anchor the changes made in the session by having a piece of labradorite and clay on her desk, and she could play with the clay, and suggested dipping her finger in honey before work. An energetic activation took place, and the higher-self told us she was accelerating her progress on the path she was on with her business.

> *There's an interesting thing that happens when we invite our client's higher consciousness to guide us to wherever the client most needs to go for understanding and transformation. And, that thing is that there appear to be multiple levels and layers of higher consciousness, and not ALL of them care about what we do for a career. Sounds kind of funny, I know, but I've encountered aspects of higher consciousness that are farther removed or more distant from the fractal of our consciousness currently operating these 3D human bodies, and have found that those are great at helping us understand and make changes at the soul level, but things like career choice or prosperity or relationships and such are viewed as trivial pursuits, temporary, just little lessons to learn along the way and not worthy of much attention. This is the aspect of our higher consciousness that seems more plugged into the collective consciousness, such that we can ask it questions of great historical importance or even receive prophetic suggestions.*

Carolyn clearly called upon just the right aspect of her client's higher consciousness for this particular task, though. The part of the higher consciousness that is considered, and often called, the highest-self, which cares very much about our earthly plight, is the best aspect or level of consciousness to ask for help from in matters of career, relationships, physical healing, prosperity and abundance, geographical location and relocation, etc.

~Kryssa

Reprogramming Perfectionism

By Carolyn Mather

This client wanted to release the need to be perfect in work and be able to remain calm and confident in work. She wanted to change her mindset to be able to focus on all the good things, not just the things they feels they don't do so well. To see anything they currently view as a negative as a learning opportunity, not to catastrophise, and to feel useless. To enjoy the challenge of work and not have excessive stress. To be able to have more positive relationships with colleagues and ultimately have a better work-life balance.

We asked the Higher-Self to go where it needed to, and to do whatever it needed. The higher-self explained that it took out a 'black chip' from the client's brain that had been put there since they were a child, but was no longer needed. It was put there to help her survive as a child because this was the only way she could feel good enough and get the attention she needed to survive- by doing her best in school and being as perfect as she could. It was the only thing she was good at and that she liked about herself.

A new chip was then put in for motivation and excitement. She gained the wisdom that she does not need to try to be perfect now, as she is in a job where there isn't always a definite right or wrong answer, and there are many opportunities to expand knowledge and continue to learn, as it is a complex job with often no black and white answer.

She realised this is an exciting job that allows her to keep developing and learning all the time. Her higher-self performed 'scans' and identified tension through her whole body, and then 'loosened' this by 'kneading it like dough and softening it', and as this happened, she felt herself expand, and felt that if she were loosened, softened and expanded she could then see more of the big picture and stop seeking an end goal of perfection which does not exist.

She also recognised that when she was a child, it was easier to strive for perfection and to achieve it, as the exams and tests they did then were simpler and often had a right or wrong answer, but the job she is in now is a different setup, so absolute perfection in it can't be attained.

We asked if there was anything else the higher-self needed to do, and it sprinkled glitter all over the client to give her her sparkle back. It told her she can put her work 'stuff' in a basket at the end of the working day and come back to it the next day, and told them what colours are best for her to wear.

As always, we asked the higher-self to fully install, integrate, and activate all wisdom and changes on every level for the client's highest good. We also asked if it is in the client's highest good to increase the percentage of connection with her higher-self, which they agreed to do. We asked what can be done to better maintain the connection with the Higher-Self, which in this case was just to know they are there and can ask for help if they need to. QJH is just amazing, I love seeing what the Higher-Self can come up with!

Imagine an entire lifetime of perfectionism, and its painful side effects of being chronically self-critical and never, ever feeling good enough, can be resolved in a single session by simply removing the old programming, acknowledging why it was there in the first place and how helpful and necessary it once was, then upgrading to new, more beneficial programming.

This is a wonderful example of how working with multiple levels and layers of consciousness simultaneously can bring about very rapid, yet very profound changes. In this case, the subconscious had placed the original programming as a protective measure in childhood. This is very common, and where most unwanted behaviors and beliefs come from. But working with the higher-self, too, the part that was able to shed light on the bigger picture and remove the old programming, is where the client got true freedom.

~Kryssa

Reigniting Psychic Talents and Holding onto a Bad Habit

By Nikki Hoare

Paul (Not his real name) had a past life regression about two years ago. He wanted to stop smoking, but he also suffers from colitis. Whilst he smokes, he doesn't experience any symptoms from the colitis. The doctors are not sure why this is. He wanted to see if there had been any changes that would allow him to stop smoking without the colitis coming back. He also wanted to find out if there was any reason why his family was having so much bad luck, so many things going wrong for the females in his family.

I thought it might be good to do an Ego State transformation in regard to the colitis, then see what guidance his highest consciousness gave. Maybe visiting the healing temple and speaking with his inner healer to resolve any issues with the colitis will then allow him to stop smoking.

As ego state transformation does not require a deep state of trance, I started with a simple focus breathing to bring a state of relaxation.

Paul went into a trance very easily. I guided him to contact that part that has anything to do with the colitis; instead, another part, also called the ego state, came through. This part said, "Paul should not worry about his colitis as it would not harm him, nor would the smoking." I felt this was actually Paul's highest consciousness, with which I was communicating. I asked what its name was and what it wished to be known by. It simply said that it had no name that Paul or I would understand.

His highest consciousness then went on to say, "Paul's colitis and smoking were for a reason. They stopped him from knowing his true purpose, as he was not ready yet. When the time is right, you will see that Paul is here for a reason. He will do great things. The world needs him, but it is not time yet."

The highest consciousness did not know why so much bad luck had fallen on his family at this time, "It is simply bad luck and will pass. He is strong."

It also wanted Paul to know that "Unfortunately, their dog is very ill and will die. The idea they have been thinking about moving is a good one. It will be better for the whole family. Also, Paul should not take the option of the steroids that the doctor wants him to take. This is not right for him."

I asked his highest consciousness if there was any way that it could still protect Paul and guide him to his future, but allow him to be free of colitis and smoking, as neither of these was good for Paul's physical body. It stated, "Paul does not need to worry about either the colitis or the smoking. They will not harm him, and I will make sure of that. But he needs them to stop him from hearing the others, for he is a beacon, and they will come, and Paul is not ready for that, not yet."

I asked if it had any words of wisdom, guidance, or support for Paul.

"He simply needs to relax, not worry so much. Everything will be fine. He can do his mediumship at the psychic group. He is good at that. Keep reading the energies – he will get better at it...When it is time to come online, he will be fine."

I asked if it would speak with the creative part of Paul, the part that has ideas and solves problems, his imaginative and creative self. And come up with new ways and ideas for Paul to be able to relax and worry less, ways that are in his highest good for the here and now. It agreed, and a few minutes later, it said, "It is done."

After confirming there was nothing else to be done for Paul's highest good at this time, I ended the session.

When Paul came out of trance, he was surprised at just how quickly his highest consciousness had come forward. It did not surprise him with the response, and that some things are not meant to be changed yet.

We discussed some of the sessions, the ideas, and suggestions the highest consciousness had, and we both agreed that any further sessions would not be of benefit to Paul at this time.

I imagine this session is going to rankle some people. Specifically, people who have either quit smoking themselves or helped others to quit smoking, and are of the belief that it is always bad for all people all of the time. And yet here is a client's higher consciousness saying not to worry about it. Perhaps you are skeptical that this event was this client's higher consciousness. And there's no way for you to qualify that...only the client can.

But I will tell you that I've run into this before. And interestingly, it was another client with natural mediumship and trance channeling abilities. In her case, the highest consciousness came through and said that the tobacco was helping to keep her energy grounded. She had switched to healthier, high-end, roll-your-own tobacco, so it wasn't laced with all the additives and chemicals of pre-rolled, boxed cigarettes. Her higher consciousness told her that was fine.

It had something to do with traversing the astral plane while channeling and needing the frequency or vibration of the tobacco to keep her tethered to her body. It also said that it would make sure that it had no negative effects on her lungs or her body and that she would never become physically addicted. She would know when and when not to use it as a tool for very specific purposes.

When I had that session, I found myself skeptical because I had been trained (brainwashed) from an early age to view smoking as unhealthy at the very least, and as an act of such great shame that anyone who does it must be a weak-willed, self-destructive, callous person who didn't care about themselves or others (second-hand smoke). When I became a hypnotist, this programming *was emphasized even more. But I had a deep, dark, secret...every once in a while, I smoked too!*

After having this session and then reading about Nikki's session above, I feel fairly certain that my own occasional tobacco use is along a similar trajectory. It's never been consistent, never daily. Not even weekly, and sometimes months or even years will pass without even thinking about it. So obviously, no addiction to worry about. But the same part? Oh yeah. I absorbed that. And I am here to say that the amount of shame I heaped upon myself via my perceived (and real) judgement from others- especially colleagues- was FAR MORE damaging than any occasional cigarette!

At the end of the day, we cannot possibly know what another's path is. Most of us barely know our own path, so if you find that something works great for you, please enjoy it to the fullest. But that doesn't give any of us the right to impose what works for us upon anyone else. This includes perceived bad habits.

We are all here for our own purposes. Let's support each other along the way, rather than shame each other. Shame causes more illness than any single bad habit on its own.

~Kryssa

The Witch and Her Father

By Ruthie Ann Yielding

Janis first came to me for allergies that have disturbed her since she was six years old. She lived by the sea and had a lot of vegetation around her home. She loved working in the garden but had terrible allergies, which limited her time working and doing the things she enjoyed out in nature. Springtime was the worst period of all.

This was her very first hypnosis session, and she was a bit agitated, so I assured her that her Highest Consciousness and I were there with her and she was completely safe. She took a few deep breaths and felt better.

She noticed a door that was calling out to her, and when she went through the door, she noticed some tall pine trees, and as she navigated further, she perceived the presence of her Inner Healer on her left side. It was an elderly woman with long hair. Her name was Michelle. We asked Michelle to help us understand why the client had these horrific allergies. Michelle said the word, "Love." I asked Michelle to explain, and she said the client had to learn to love herself more. I asked Michelle in which ways Janis could show more self-love, but Janis could not hear the answer.

Further digging into the allergy issue, Michelle told us that the issue was from a previous life. I asked if she was willing to come with us to this past life, and she said she would come with us, but she needed help. So, we called upon any other helpers or guides, and Archangel Gabriel came to us. Archangel Gabriel told us that Janis had to free herself from the weight of a past life. I asked what this weight was. Archangel Gabriel said it came forth from a death...the death of her father (in another life), but in this life, her father is alive. But Janis says that when she thinks about her father, she feels a grey cloud over his life.

She began to tell me about a dream she had when she was very small (6-7 years old) that left her a bit traumatized. She said they were walking on the road, and there was a person who was faking being ill or hurt. When her father went there to help the person, the person stabbed him.

Then she told me that just a few nights before our session, she had dreamed that her father had fallen down from the roof of their home (she still lives at home). I asked her how she felt about that dream, and she said that she felt like it was her fault that she couldn't help him or stop him from falling. Delving deeper into these dreams, I discovered that the first dream left her almost breathless...she was literally having difficulty breathing. I worked with her on this because she felt as if she was suffocating.

Archangel Gabriel said that this dream, but not only this dream, is one of the reasons behind her allergies. And that the root problem was in another life. Janis immediately felt herself floating up, and I assured her that we were all with her...her Higher Consciousness, Michelle, Archangel Gabriel, and myself.

She found herself in a green field, and the sensation she felt was of being a little out of sorts. In this place, she could breathe without problems. It was daytime, and she was dressed in medieval clothing. She had on a light brown leather skirt and a rough-textured shirt.

All of a sudden, she felt the thundering of horses vibrate the earth under her feet. She then saw many men galloping past her. They were headed into the forest to her left, and she could see a village in the opposite direction. I encouraged her to go towards the village, and she found herself outside the tall village walls. She immediately felt uncomfortable that she couldn't see the entrance, and she felt extremely distressed when she saw the horsemen that had previously galloped by her so abruptly. They scared her. She felt as if they were searching for someone.

She found herself in a room with someone on a throne in front of her, while she was there on her knees with her arms tied behind her back. She felt that she was being condemned, and looking around, she saw other people on their knees beside her. Suddenly, she saw her father in that life. At that moment, she realized that all the people on their knees were being condemned for being witches. She expressed feelings of sadness, worry, and fear. Then she began to cry. We called upon Archangel Michael.

Janis and her father lived outside the village. They were dressed like poor people who lived in the forest, exactly where the men on the horses were riding. Janis said they were being condemned for things that they did not do…for being witches.

I instructed Janis to go back in time to that moment when the men on the horses arrived in the forest and tell me what was happening. She said she was cooking things that they had gathered from the forest. The men on the horses arrived, threw everything on the ground, and then took them back to the village. She felt so afraid. I asked her what she felt about this fear that she was experiencing, and she said it was connected to the feeling of being impotent and was directly connected to her allergies and the sense of being responsible for her father's life in her present life.

Archangel Michael severed the cords from this lifetime to that lifetime with Archangels Gabriel and Michael and Inner Healer Michelle to let Janis take all the lessons from this experience that would serve her and leave the trauma behind. She began to cry when the cord was cut…she was holding the cord. She felt liberated. We thanked Archangels Gabriel and Michael for their assistance.

Direct lines of communication with her Inner Healer, Michelle, were opened and anchored so she could call upon her anytime now.

Janis awakened with a new outlook on her life, and she is now looking forward to Spring.

Recovering from allergies is well within the reach of hypnosis as long as it's safe for the client to release them. However, there is no one-size-fits-all approach. For some, like Janis, the issues stem from a past life. For others, it could be the remnants of a parental introject, or a way for the body to alert the person that an imbalance needs to be addressed, which would be the more traditional, physiologically based histamine response. And sometimes it's not necessary to go back to the origins in order to release the allergies...but since we as practitioners don't know what the client needs MORE than their higher consciousness knows, despite our collections of skills, tools, desire to show them off, etc., in QJH we stick with just asking to be led wherever the client most needs to go in order to address their issue. Because it's not us as practitioners making assumptions about our clients' care, it takes quite a bit of pressure off our ego to have to approach our sessions performatively.

~Kryssa

Embracing the Depths: A Journey of Connection and Healing

By Ruthie Ann Yielding

In the vast expanse of the subconscious lies a realm where past, present, and future intertwine—a realm where profound healing and enlightenment await those brave enough to venture forth. In the case study of "Embracing the Depths," we embark on a transformative journey of self-discovery and connection with Janis once again, guided by the wisdom of the subconscious mind and the nurturing embrace of divine beings. The session unfolds as the client, seeking resolution for persistent allergies, finds herself transported to the Hallway of Answers—a realm that she found shrouded in darkness save for the luminescent glow of white doors.

Guided by the practitioner, she is drawn towards a door that beckons her with its enigmatic allure, leading her into the verdant embrace of a forest teeming with life. Here, she encounters her Inner Healer, Michelle, who serves as a beacon of guidance and support on her journey of healing. Through the gentle probing of the practitioner, Michelle unveils the deep-seated roots of the client's allergies—a poignant connection to childhood trauma and the suffocating expectations of perfection imposed by her mother.

With compassionate guidance, Michelle releases the client from the grip of past trauma, severing the ties that bound her to the sensation of asphyxiation and liberating her from the weight of unrealized expectations. In a moment of profound healing, Michelle facilitates a cleansing Light Energy Shower, purifying the client's energetic and physical body of any lingering negativity or discomfort.

A comprehensive hypnotic body scan reveals and addresses lingering physical ailments, furthering the process of holistic restoration and renewal. With newfound clarity and connection to her Inner Healer, the client embarks on a journey of self-empowerment and liberation, guided by the wisdom of her Highest Consciousness, Agnia.

Through a deep dive into the depths of her subconscious, she discovers a profound connection to the element of water—a bond forged in a past life as an agile swimmer, enveloped in the tranquil embrace of the lake's depths. Embracing the wisdom imparted by Agnia, the client emerges from the session with a sense of profound clarity and purpose, empowered to follow her dreams and embrace her authentic self without fear of judgment or perfectionism.

Anchoring the lessons learned and the healing received, she returns to her waking consciousness with a renewed sense of strength, tranquility, and self-assurance. The case study of Embracing the Depths stands as a testament to the transformative power of Quantum Journeys Hypnosis in unlocking the hidden depths of the subconscious mind, facilitating profound healing, and guiding individuals toward a path of self-discovery, empowerment, and enlightenment. Through courage, compassion, and connection, individuals can embark on a journey of profound transformation, embracing the boundless possibilities that lie within.

When QJH practitioners mention "anchoring," they are referring to a hypnotic process where we ask the client, while in a trance state, to bring the change into them and associate it with something that can bring it to the forefront whenever needed. This might be a physical gesture, like clasping their hands together, or it might be associating it with a color or a word. The important part is that the client comes up with the idea themselves.

Another thing we do is activate the new programming they've just installed and integrated. It isn't particularly helpful to only install it if it isn't then activated.

~Kryssa

Jasmine in the Realm of Orange and the Beanstalk

By Ruthie Ann Yielding

Jasmine sought guidance through Quantum Journeys Hypnosis to explore her inner landscape and clarify her life's path. She embarked on a transformative journey where she encountered profound revelations in the form of metaphors and wisdom from her Highest Consciousness. Reaching the Hallway of Answers, Jasmine described her hallway as a long tunnel flowing through a black hole in the sky.

The energy was everywhere, circulating through this tunnel, and it felt like basic primordial energy. Guiding her attention towards the Hallway, she noticed a light towards the left that was calling her attention. I suggested going towards the light, and she advised me that she would have to step through the light. She did so and described it as a feeling of empty space, like a parallel universe, but with nothing in it. I asked to allow her eyes to adjust to this frequency.

After adjusting her eyes to this frequency, she encountered a majestic waterfall, and at the base, there was a verdant oasis adorned with mushrooms…Big mushrooms with strong roots. She then got a nudge from something, or just a sense to pick up the mushroom. She attempted to do so but couldn't because it's attached to the location…it had strong roots. Amidst this surreal tableau, Jasmine's journey took an unexpected turn as she encountered her Highest Consciousness in the form of a tarantula…an unexpected and whimsical manifestation.

Hesitant to accept this as her Highest Consciousness, she soon found herself captivated by the creature's wisdom and grace. Transforming its hairy legs into what resembled delicate flower petals, dancing gracefully amidst the cosmic ballet right there before her eyes, before morphing into a radiant entity named Orange, which revealed itself as a beacon of enlightenment, guiding Jasmine towards profound revelations and inner transformation. Orange displayed a red spear adorned with a Fleur de Lis, symbolizing courage and clarity in the face of adversity.

Through this powerful metaphor for dispelling hindrances and embracing empowerment, Jasmine discovered the strength to overcome obstacles, such as limiting beliefs, and navigate the winding path of her destiny. Inquisitive about her potential for healing, Jasmine was met with a tapestry of botanical imagery, symbolizing the inherent power within nature. Orange emphasized the significance of embracing one's gifts without burden, nurturing them with intention and mindfulness.

Through the metaphor of illumination, Orange encouraged Jasmine to shine brightly, harnessing her innate abilities to channel and multiply energies for healing, not only for others but also for herself. Amidst the beauty and wonder of the subconscious realm, Jasmine confronted her own resistance to praise and self-worth. Through Orange's gentle guidance, she began to unravel the layers of generational conditioning and societal expectations that had held her back, learning to embrace transparency, her true essence, and resilience to shine brightly as a beacon of light in the darkness.

Jasmine learned to deflect negative energies and protect her inner sanctum from external influences, embodying a newfound sense of empowerment and self-worth. Orange disclosed to Jasmine, "You are on the right path. When you feel there is a nudge…that's a seed growing up…. that's going to become something beautiful. Stay focused and don't allow your attention to go astray. Just be aware of the seeds."

With Orange's guidance, Jasmine discovered the importance of keeping the lines of communication open, symbolized by the growing beanstalk…a reminder to look upwards, reach upwards, and connect with her Highest Consciousness. After thanking Orange for all the wisdom and guidance she had given, we turned to make our way back into the Hallway of Answers.

However, Jasmine decided she would take a different path…a new path where she would take with her all the lessons learned and the assurance that she is part of something greater, ready to embrace her journey with courage and resilience and knowing that the bean-stalk metaphor served as a powerful reminder to continue reaching upward, nurturing her potential, and connecting with her Highest Consciousness for guidance and support on her life's journey.

These sorts of free exploration of the Hallway of Answers sessions are so fun for both the client and the practitioner! I liken them to those old Choose-Your-Own-Adventure books. We never know where we're going to be guided or what and who we'll encounter, but it's always empowering and always transformational.

One thing you may have noticed by now is that the higher consciousness doesn't perceive its job as having anything to do with making our lives easier or less challenging. They are available to help us navigate through the rough patches in order to collect the necessary wisdom through the various experiences we seemingly signed up for, but like a doting grandparent, they're not interested in swooping and saving us. That would defeat the entire purpose of being here…of being alive.

~Kryssa

Dead Man Walking 1809

By Ruthie Ann Yielding

In this anthology report, we will explore the original transcript of a session involving a client who sought help for allergies, sciatica pain, left shoulder nerve pain, and post-nasal drip. The session involved visualization exercises and communication with the client's inner healer. The client also addressed her fear of uncertainty and received guidance on finding a new home.

Additionally, the session delved into a past life regression to the year 1809, where the client experienced a connection to a man walking to the gallows. The session concluded with advice on processing emotions and interacting with others.

Allergies and Sciatica Pain

The client came for a session seeking relief from allergies, sciatica pain, left shoulder nerve pain, and post-nasal drip. In a previous session, the client discovered specific tree allergies (Birch and Ash) and realised that her home was surrounded by these trees. Although she considered moving, she had not done so by the time of the second session.

Visualization Exercise

During the second session, the client had difficulty imagining a hallway but eventually visualized a narrow, tall hallway with a bright pink light shining through one of the doors. Upon entering that door, she saw a meadow with short-cut grass, resembling a paradise. She noticed a red checked blanket on the ground and encountered a red squirrel that led her to a big Oak Tree and a red door. Inside the tree, she discovered that the Oak Tree was her Temple of Healing, and the red squirrel was her Inner Healer named Red.

Addressing Physical Issues

The Inner Healer, Red, provided guidance on addressing the client's physical issues. For the sciatic nerve issue, specific exercises were recommended. The client was also advised to move more since she spent most of her time sitting. To alleviate the nerve pain in her left shoulder radiating down to her left palm, specific exercises were prescribed.

Fear of Uncertainty and Moving House

The client's fear of uncertainty regarding moving house was addressed during the session. She was instructed to follow her heart and find a place where she would be around people. The client was encouraged to be more neighborly, stop judging, take a leap, and let go of control.

Geographical Information and Promenade

Red provided the client with geographical information. The client visualized herself walking on a promenade, seeing boats, yachts, and people speaking different languages. She observed boats on the left and a line of bars, shops, and restaurants on the right side. The client also noticed outside tables with metal legs on light-colored wooden planks.

Allergies and Stress

The client inquired about acquiring natural antihistamines for her allergies. Red explained that stress worsened her allergies and advised her to relax more, spend time outdoors, and be around other people.

Past Life Regression to 1809

During the session, the client mentioned "dead man walking" and a thick rope around the neck, associating it with her allergies as a restriction preventing her from enjoying life. The client revealed that in a past life in 1809, she was a man who stole food due to hunger and was sent to the gallows as a result. The connection between this past life and the client's current life was explored.

Releasing Restrictions and Constrictions

To release the restrictions and constrictions associated with the past life, the client was guided to go to the "life between lives" and separate the connection. The client closed the connection to the old life, apologized, forgave, and sent love to heal that life. The remaining cord from the old life was placed back into that life. All cords were cut and severed, and it was determined that no further attention was needed in the 1809 lifetime.

Processing Feelings and Interacting with Others

Before concluding the session, the client expressed a desire to work on how she processes her feelings and interacts with people. Red advised her to "lean in" and allow herself to enjoy and feel her emotions. By doing so, the client could gain a more positive mindset, trust, and faith.

Red also addressed the client's discomfort with clothing high up around her neck or short-chained necklaces, suggesting that it was a sensation created in the mind and could be changed through a new mindset.

Conclusion

The session concluded with gratitude expressed to the client's Highest Consciousness and Red for their work. The client received advice on processing emotions, interacting with others, and changing her mindset. The wisdom imparted was to believe in oneself.

*Please note that the information provided in this anthology report is based on the original transcript of the session and does not constitute medical or psychological advice.

Everything that comes up in a client session has some sort of symbolic meaning or message to impart. Some of these may be universal symbols, and others will be very personal and specific to the client. This includes colors, animals, objects, places, beings, events, and features.

In this particular session the color red came up frequently. That would be highly meaningful even if it only came up once, but it came up at least three times and was the name of her Inner Healer. Red is often associated with the root chakra, or the energy center at the base of the pelvis. And that could be the case here, but it's best not to assume...especially because we can just ask.

Working with the higher consciousness is a bit different than working only with the subconscious, as you may have gathered by now. For example, we don't have to use hypnotic language and tiptoe around syntax so as not to confuse the subconscious, which tends to be quite literal in its interpretation of language, though still symbolic in its interpretation of objects and events.

In the above example, the practitioner was able to seamlessly move from one place to another with the client without having to use any tricky or slippery wordplay. Just simple, direct questions regarding what to do next for the client's highest good, where to go next for the client's highest good, and so on.

~Kryssa

Parallel Lives

By Christine Nicholson

I found this session so interesting as I had not come across parallel lives before, but this client certainly opened my eyes. I will use her own words at times.

She immediately became aware of the Highest Consciousness standing behind her, showing her a very big door in front of the left pillar, silvery-white, shiny, nearly invisible, barely revealing itself. I asked if the door had a knob or handle, and it did. She reached out her hand and turned the knob, opened the door…. Opening the door, she stepped through it and stopped for a moment. She is now outside and realises she has a 'bird's eye view' of the New Zealand countryside, hills, wild, calm, and green.

"It is daytime, just a view, I am observing. I cannot see movement apart from nature. I am standing and can smell something. I am wearing a silver-grey body suit and observing from an open, see-through, or invisible magnetic craft, and I am feeling a funny sensation in my stomach, like butterflies."

At this point, she became quiet, and I encouraged her to become aware of who she was and what she was observing.

"I am from a different Galaxy to observe while protecting and keeping an eye on a portal or health spot of the planet – observing at the ready, keeping a kind, friendly, protective eye on that spot. I am completely alone. I feel alone."

My client then explained that it is clear now that the solitude of the observation part is evident in her life and is connected to this parallel existence.

She continues, "There may be other places, but here is a reason, there can be, in the future, calmness, solitude, meditation for the awakening, knowledge, and understanding for the third eye opening in the right place. It takes solitude, nature, and calm. There are many parallel lives; between 30-50 at any given moment, although time and space do not count, but here in this clutter, I can see between 30-50 at once, although there may be many more".

I asked if she was aware of any existence in another parallel life. She confirmed that there is, and she is a male in this one, a father who abandoned his wife and children during the Irish famine, the potato famine. At this point, she took a breath and stated she believes she has an energy attachment, one which stays with her in this present life she is living, which connects with the male abandonment she is experiencing and feelings of her past of the one left behind. "It was hard days."

I asked if it was right for her higher consciousness to cut the cord between her and this male fractal of consciousness in the parallel life she was witnessing, as it was having a detrimental effect on her current incarnation, and it agreed.

My client stated she would receive downloads during meditations and in dreams within the last 12 months.

We asked for any words of wisdom or encouragement that her Higher Consciousness had for her. It said, "She must be ready for what she has to do and be confident and able when the time comes. There is change, and she will trust and remember and have all the support from her guides and us. We are close.'

"The lines are open, and she can contact guides, and when ready, she will be able to contact the higher dimension in time – time which has no meaning for us."

And then, "The sign will come, and she will feel it when she feels the trees around her. The trees will communicate with her".

At this moment, her first parallel-life self spoke up again, "It is the same. We are here for you. There is too much damage to the planet, and understanding is important. When you are ready, there will be an opening of minds, but slowly."

I would never have encountered the possibility of parallel lifetimes if not for becoming a hypnotherapist- and keeping an open mind when the first few 'woowoo' clients began describing them while in a trance state. At first, I thought that it was pretty rare, as it was only one in maybe 50 client sessions where this would come up.

Later, when I was given the opportunity to communicate with an aspect of the collective consciousness of humanity through a client who just spontaneously began channeling this large collective (a story for the next Quantum Journeys book), I was told that it's actually the opposite. It's incredibly rare for a client to NOT have multiple parallel lives. Especially in this particular timeline. The highest number I've run across was a client who tapped into her "oversoul" (her language for it), and it said there were roughly 900 incarnations all connected to that one oversoul. But we're not meant to have an emotional or energetic connection with these other lives, as far as I can tell- again, based on what my clients have told me. It can cause several issues for the client, and it seems best to cut cords between them if any accidentally exist. But, since none of us know more about what's in our clients' highest good than their own higher consciousness knows, we always ask first.

~Kryssa

Canceling a Soul Contract in the Akashic Records

By Jonathan Finn

"I facilitated a QJH Session for Sarah (Pseudonym) as she had been experiencing weight management issues for a number of years.

Her main issue was not in dropping the extra weight (which she actually found easy) but dropping it and keeping it off.

As quickly as she dropped the excess weight, she would just as quickly put it back on shortly afterward.

Despite being a skilled Practitioner in various modalities herself, Sarah struggled to get to the root of the issue and was curious to see if QJH could help.

In her QJH Session, Sarah found herself in a large, regal-looking library stacked from floor to ceiling with books. She admired this place and felt it was the Akashic Records.

As she began exploring this place, she noticed someone else there with her: a wise, older-looking man in a white robe who, at first, was looking at her quite impatiently.

As she approached this man, he revealed his name to be "John," and he introduced himself as the Guardian of the Records. His expression changed from one of impatience to joy and excitement as he explained to Sarah, he had been waiting for her to arrive for quite a while! He urged her to begin exploring the library as there was no time to waste, directing her to various books one after another, each containing guidance, downloads, or healing to serve her highest good.

However, with the last book she discovered, she finally found the answers to the weight management issues she'd been struggling with for so long. She described this last book as "Official looking with stamps and seals" and mentioned it was quite large.

As she opened this book and began making her way through it, she quickly realised this book contained all the details of her Soul Contract for her present lifetime, as Sarah (Although she was aware of only being allowed access to certain information within her Soul Contract at this time). As she read, she came to one particular page that finally answered her burning question about her weight management issues.

This page explained that when creating her Soul Contract before incarnating, she wished to experience and develop the ability to take on others' energies in order to transmute them. However, this plan hadn't been working out as smoothly as intended for Sarah. She learned that she had actually been taking on much more of other people's energies than she could safely handle.

As a result, she had been carrying this excess "energetic weight", which in turn continued manifesting as the physical weight she'd been struggling to keep off!

This was a light bulb moment for Sarah and made perfect sense as to why she couldn't keep the excess weight off in the past.

After finishing the rest of the book, we called forth Sarah's "Higher-Self" and asked if it was in her highest good to alter or revoke this part of her Soul Contract, as it had been negatively affecting different areas of her life.

With a "Yes" from Sarah's Higher-Self, she got the go-ahead to remove this agreement from the book containing her Soul Contract.

Sarah tore the page out of the book and decided she wanted to burn this part of the contract in a nearby rubbish bin. She put the page in the rubbish bin, excited to burn it and finally be free of this issue. She gasped as the page simply disappeared from the bin before her eyes!

Before leaving the library, she received confirmation that this agreement was indeed removed and revoked from her Soul Contract. She just didn't have to resort to burning it!

Sarah was very happy with what she'd received, changed, and discovered in her QJH Session and was really looking forward to keeping the excess weight off."

I absolutely adore it when clients discover that their very real 3D human issues can be resolved through communication with our multidimensional consciousness. Many people mistakenly think that Quantum Healing or 'spiritual hypnosis' is only useful for exploration or mind expansion. And while exploration and mind expansion can be fun, it isn't necessarily helpful to us with our daily human struggles and plights. I mean, it's all well and good to discover that you are a Starseed, for example (someone with origins on another planet or star system), but how does that benefit the human that they are in the here and now?

Quantum Journeys Hypnosis is a protocol that bridges the esoteric with the existential, so we can get real transformations that benefit ourselves and our clients today, in this lifetime, while also resolving the unseen issues that may be contributing to the problem from other aspects of our consciousness.

~Kryssa

Clearing Trapped Energy

By Jonathan Finn

"Angela (Pseudonym) contacted me as she had been struggling with issues of Self-Worth, particularly around not feeling "good enough", being unable to trust herself, and being afraid to advertise and step into her business.

These issues have affected both her personal everyday life and her new business.

In our first QJH Session together, Angela was guided to visit the "Temple of Healing", where she connected with her "Inner Healer," a tall, powerful woman named Nazeer.

Nazeer got right to work, sharing some valuable insights with Angela before performing a Body Scan on her physical and energetic bodies, identifying, explaining, and clearing anything that did not serve her highest good.

Nazeer explained to Angela that she had accumulated many years' worth of trapped energy and density, which was being held in her physical body, especially in her back.

As the clearing and releasing of this dense energy took place, Angela noted strong tingling sensations throughout her entire body, particularly in her arms and hands.

Angela was surprised when Nazeer told her that it was actually Angela herself who was doing the healing!

After clearing the physical blockages, Nazeer gently guided Angela back through various old memories that were holding her back, helping her to re-assess and release any painful, negative emotions attached to them.

Finally, Nazeer helped Angela by letting her know the best ways to continue communicating with her in the future and giving her some more valuable advice for moving forward on her path to fulfill her life purpose.

Before leaving the Temple of Healing, Nazeer decided to give Angela one final parting message.

"Don't judge yourself so harshly. You can always address things at the moment instead of looking back on them. Remember your purpose."

Angela came back to the present time feeling much lighter and freer, as if a huge weight had been lifted off her shoulders.

She was now deeply aware of what had been holding her back and, more importantly, at peace with it and free from the pain it had been causing her.

Angela reported rapid, positive shifts after our QJH Sessions together, stating her overall well-being has improved and that there are big changes in how she sees things and how she shows up for herself in daily life.

Angela is now thriving personally as well as in her business, happily advertising her work and abilities, knowing she's fulfilling her life purpose."

> *This is a beautiful example of the basic foundation of healing that Quantum Journeys Hypnosis offers clients. To give them the understanding that they are enough, that they are supported, that they are worthy, and quite capable of healing themselves are all life-changing and yet almost guaranteed to occur in just about every session. It's not something we, as practitioners, even have to request within the session…it is freely offered by the client's own higher consciousness, often in the form of their Inner Healer.*

> *~Kryssa*

Past Life Trauma and Current Life Phobia

By Jonathan Finn

"Caroline (Pseudonym) contacted me seeking help in overcoming an intense fear of sharing a room with others at night-time. This consuming fear had been greatly affecting her quality of life for many years, preventing her from travelling and going on trips away with friends, family, etc. Caroline had had this issue since late childhood (now in her mid-30s) and had spent a lot of time and money on other therapies to address and overcome this fear with no success.

In our initial session, Caroline wondered if perhaps an incident of physical abuse may be at the root of this intense fear, although she stated she had no recollection of any kind of abuse from her childhood. However, we both agreed to allow her "Higher-Self" to call forth and guide her to whatever experiences were most appropriate to address this issue for good. I facilitated two QJH Sessions with Caroline on this particular issue. Her first session consisted of revisiting and healing certain childhood events.

Caroline noticed some positive shifts in herself and felt lighter after her first Session.

However, it was during her second QJH session that we encountered a breakthrough with the issue. After being guided to the most appropriate experience by her "Higher-Self", I asked her to describe her surroundings, and she noticed an older, weathered-looking woman standing off to her left. Caroline described her as looking like she was from "the olden days with big hair".

I asked Caroline if it was possible for her to communicate with this woman, and she answered "Yes". I then had her ask this woman who she was, and unexpectedly, she revealed herself to be Caroline from a Past Lifetime!

This encounter was an unexpected twist in the Session and then begged the question: what does this centuries-old Past Life of Caroline's have to do with the overwhelming fear she's been experiencing?

After further questioning, we discovered that this woman had actually been hanging around Caroline for quite a while in an attempt to protect her and keep her safe.

The woman explained that the reason she was doing this was not because of any negative events from

Caroline's present life but because of negative events that happened in Caroline's past lifetime when she lived as this woman.

We also learned that the intense fear Caroline felt when sharing rooms with others had nothing to do with any events from her present lifetime. This fear stemmed from traumas she'd experienced in her Past Lifetime as that woman, which had lain dormant at a Soul level. By coming forward, her energetic presence was unconsciously picked up by Caroline, causing the past-life fears and traumas to be re-triggered for her, resulting in the fear she'd been struggling with ever since.

After speaking with this woman further and explaining the impact this was having on Caroline's well-being, she understood that, despite her best intentions, her presence in Caroline's life was ultimately hindering her instead of helping her.

When she realised this, she was apologetic and willing to move on, knowing that she'd done all she could to help Caroline, and it was now time to move on to the Light.

We called forward Caroline's "Higher-Self" to assist the well-meaning Past Life woman towards the Light, where she could continue her own journey to find peace and healing from the negative events of that lifetime. Following her second QJH Session, Caroline happily reported there had been some profound shifts in her life.

Not only had that intense fear of 20+ years disappeared, but she also said that she felt much lighter and happier overall, stating, "a huge weight has lifted".

Her family had also noticed the positive changes in Caroline, which she took as an extra confirmation of the powerful shifts that had taken place!

It is not uncommon to have a first session be all about gently peeling back the layers of old, blocked traumas that may be interfering with the client moving into a new perception or way of being. Inner child rescue work is often a necessary first step.

But rather than approaching any session with a plan to do this or that or something else, we enter into a collaboration with the aspects of the client that know exactly what they need, and then we simply ask how we may assist.

In the second session, we encounter the power of a past life personality, which can take on energy that feels similar to an attached entity—even though it's simply the vestiges of an unresolved personality. Jonathan did a fantastic job of helping to resolve the issue that was keeping this particular past-life personality stuck and allowing the client to shed decades' worth of intense fear.

~Kryssa

Feels Like Home

By Jonathan Finn

Brianna (Pseudonym) got in touch with me seeking to release strong feelings of unworthiness and low self-esteem, as well as some general negativity from recent events in her life that had been weighing her down and affecting both her personal and professional life.

Brianna said her main goal was to become more confident, more loving of herself, and more open to receiving love.

During her first QJH Session, Brianna found herself being guided down a long tunnel with a bright light at the very end. When she emerged at the other end, she found herself in a blissful place of pure, overwhelming love.

I've had numerous clients visit this awe-inspiring place in the past, and interestingly, they all describe it in the same way or very similarly. This place is often referred to as "Source", although it can go by many different names, such as "Oneness" or "All that is".

As Brianna entered this place, she showed visible signs of feeling this overwhelming love and began describing her experience.

Below is a transcript of Brianna's profound experience entering this place:

Practitioner (P): What do you notice around you now? Have you come out the other end, or are you still in that tunnel?

Brianna (B): It's just so much overwhelming love here.

(P): Overwhelming love. Beautiful. Can you describe that place to me?

(B): It's…it's an empty space. Nothing…nothing is there but…just… just one love.

Brianna was smiling brightly and let out a loud sigh.

(P): So, there's nothing there then, just that feeling of love?

(B): Just that feeling.

(P): Sounds beautiful…How does that feel now?

(B): They were waiting for me. They were waiting for me for a long time.

(P): Wow! And you're finally there.

(B): I'm finally there.

(P): How does that feel?

(B): It feels like home.

Brianna became visibly emotional at this point.

(P): Feels like home, that's OK, and just allow yourself to feel that beautiful feeling of home and love in that place now. You mentioned they were waiting for you. Did you get a sense of who was waiting for you?

(B): It's…it's my Higher-Self. We meet again.

(P): Do you get any sense or feeling from your Higher-Self?

(B): I just feel it…

(P): Wonderful. You can just continue to feel that now, knowing that you're finally there.

(B): I'm finally there…

(P): That's right. So now that you're there, do you get a sense of anything else in this place, or is it just the feeling?

(B): It's a feeling, but there is more; it's just not one… there are so many entities…there's a group of collective beings just on the other side…

Brianna had difficulty articulating her experience here.

(P): Ok, so there are other beings in that place, too?

(B): They're all loving...

(P): Do you get a sense of who they are, or do you recognise any of them?

(B): They're just lights. I see light. Just heads of light...

At this point, Brianna's Higher-Self began communicating directly through her and proceeded to give insights and answers around the issues she wished to address, as well as healing some minor health issues she'd been facing.

Brianna received a lot of information and guidance from her Higher-Self, much of which cannot be shared due to being deeply personal. However, this was the parting message her Higher-Self offered before we wrapped up the Session.

"She's healed. She's healed from her health issues, and all is clear. She will help a lot of people. She will be super busy. She will help a lot of people through her intention."

After coming back out of hypnosis, Brianna began to recount her experience of the unconditional love she felt, but she still had difficulty describing just how profound her experience was.

> *This incredible place that several of our clients find themselves in seems to be the same- or similar- place that I found myself in during my first Near Death Experience (and many times in the past few years). If I'd only known then that I could visit anytime I need to, simply by going into a state of trance, then I might have prevented the 3 decades of depression that followed.*
>
> *QJH clients describe it as feeling full of unconditional love, support, wisdom, and peace…I described it as "home".*
>
> *Hypnotherapist and author Michael Newton calls it the Life Between Lives. Others call it the Afterlife.*
>
> *Whatever this place is, we seem to be familiar with it. As if we knew it existed without having any conscious awareness or memory of it until we find ourselves there again, and then it's like "Ahhhh! Right. I kind of remember this".*

If you get the chance to visit, I highly recommend you do so...but please don't almost die for your transport. There's a much easier and less invasive route: Quantum Journeys Hypnosis.

~Kryssa

Baby Charly Receives Support

By Henriette Kern-Schuh

One of my clients, a man of 54 years named Charly, came to see me because of very low self-esteem, anxieties, and fear of not being good enough and of making wrong decisions. His goals were to have more self-confidence, more stability in his private life and job, and to be able to face challenges and stand strong.

At first, we worked on numerous hindering and limiting beliefs about himself. I have a long list of such beliefs, like "I am not good enough", "I'm not lovable", "I'm not worth being loved", "I do everything wrong", etc. Many people have such unconscious beliefs, which they have formed during their life, mainly in childhood, when they hear them from parents, teachers, or other authorities. I find the right ones using the kinesiologic o-ring test and then solve them either by EFT (emotional freedom technique) or EMDR (eye movement desensitization and reprocessing).

Then I decided to do hypnosis with him in order to get an idea of where his anxieties came from.

I had him call his Higher-Self to ask for assistance. He described it as a slim, transparent dash. At first, there was a kind of muddle of images that dissolved after a time. Suddenly, Charly felt hope and reassurance that he could let go of the past and be happy again soon. As we all have lots of ego states or so-called inner parts within our minds, which all have a certain task to fulfill for our highest good, I asked him to call his anxiety part. It appeared in the form of a baby, which was also its name. The insight was that the baby was alone, helpless, and in need of secureness and confidence. The anxiety made it cry, which was useful, of course, at that age, as its mother came running to calm it.

We called an Inner Helper to give Baby confidence. We kind of reconditioned Baby, telling it that in the meantime, Charly was a grown-up man, and that anxiety was not helpful anymore because he could help himself now. To our surprise, Baby changed its appearance to a big tree with strong roots, standing in the client's wonderful garden. At once, Charly felt strong, stable, and independent, as if he were able to take care of himself. We anchored these emotions again with the two fingers of his left hand.

The very next day, he let me know he was feeling much more relaxed and self-assured. I love these QJH techniques, which can so easily help clients feel the way they want to.

> *One thing I really love about QJH is how seamlessly it intertwines with other modalities at pretty much any point in the session, from the intake to the pretalk to the induction to the deeper trance work to the emergence. If you have other tools and skills you've acquired along your own academic path, please bring them!*
>
> *I realize this is pretty unusual in the realm of trainers in my profession, but I firmly believe that each student who resonates with this training is meant to bring their own flavor to it and then go out into the world and find those clients that resonate with that new flavor fusion. No two QJH practitioners are ever going to conduct sessions in exactly the same way, and I designed it to be that way very much on purpose.*
>
> *We all have gifts and talents that emerge over time as a result of utilizing all that we've*

learned and are learning, and integrating ancient knowledge we reacquire as well. We are intended to bring exactly who we are in our most authentic ways to the world at large, and I do not have the right to demand that anyone adhere strictly to only MY WAY, as if my way is somehow superior to all other ways. The clients who are meant to find me and benefit from my way of doing things will. And the clients that are meant to find other practitioners or even other modalities will find who and what they need when they need them.

~Kryssa

The Unexpected Helper

By Henriette Kern-Schuh

My first session after completing the live training was with Mary, a client who had come to me in order to improve her self-confidence, courage, and independence.

I hadn't worked with hypnosis with her before. That's why I wondered how it would be because she's quite analytical. But everything worked well.

At first, she found herself in a splendid Hallway of answers with many doors. Behind one of the doors, she saw some light shining through, so she knew which one to choose. She entered the room, which was full of light, but it was completely empty. On the other side, there was a window door to a balcony. From there, she could look down into a wonderful garden - but only look because there was no way to reach it from the balcony. She concluded later that the garden represented all the beautiful places she didn't have access to because of her lack of self-confidence and courage.

Back inside the empty room, we called her Higher-Self, which appeared in the form of a big bird, like a hawk, but it just looked at her and didn't give any advice. I gave Mary some time to explore the room more thoroughly. Finally, she found a mirror on one of the walls. There, she saw her Inner Child (around 3 or 4 years old). The little girl seemed to be quite happy, open-minded, and curious.

In most cases, the inner child needs some reassurance from the adult. This situation seemed to be the other way around. The child was quite confident and could give some of her abilities and qualities to the woman who had lost them somewhere along the way.

Both had an enlightening conversation about confidence, self-love, and curiosity. Furthermore, little Mary told the adult to forgive and make peace with her mother, with whom she had broken off contact for some years already.

Looking around the room, Mary found a smaller mirror with her mother's face. This led to a nice and understanding conversation between the two women.

At last, Mary went back to the mirror with little Mary. She seemed to be a bit older now and looked very satisfied with my client, who felt full of love, serenity, and confidence.

I made her send this love from heart to heart and back, and both of them enjoyed it a lot.

After they had said goodbye till the next encounter, I slowly emerged Mary from the hypnosis. She felt really happy and was looking forward to the changes to come.

There are a lot of different varieties of Inner Child Rescue work in the fields of psychotherapy, psychology, hypnotherapy, and hypnosis, but what a revelation to have the pure joy of the Inner Child to rescue the adult who forgot how to experience pure joy.

As you've no doubt noticed by now, one of the most prevalent issues people seek our help for is not feeling worthy or good enough. It comes in a variety of different packages— perfectionism, not feeling loveable, having abandonment or rejection wounds, social anxiety, fear of commitment, impossible standards, inability to accept oneself, etc.

But the approach is still to always ask the client's own higher-self to reveal where we need to go and what we need to do to create a sense of balance. To "release resistance" to feeling good. We all began life feeling pretty good, so we can consider that our default setting. Then it's just a matter of peeling back the layers of subconscious protective stuff we've picked up along the way- the stuff that's been masquerading as coping mechanisms and sabotaging behaviors and revealing the core truth that is at the center of each of us. LOVE.

~Kryssa

Three Sessions and a Whole Life Transformation

By Lisa Morgan

Louise had been a coaching client of mine for around three months before I introduced QJH into our sessions, and it became a game-changer. I met her at a retreat I was facilitating, and we clicked immediately. Within one week of the meeting, she had signed up for a 6-month coaching program for self-empowerment. When we met, Louise did not seem overly spiritual, so I used more traditional hypnosis and life coaching methods in our sessions. I did, however, sprinkle in a little more 'woo' each week. At the end of three months, she had developed a deep trust in me and was excited to experience a different method of hypnosis that not only tapped into her subconscious but also her higher consciousness.

I could not believe what she connected with in our sessions. Here is an insight into Louise's journey. As mentioned, Louise originally signed up with me because she felt lost. She was about to retire and needed direction. After a couple of months of working together, our focus changed to her selling her business that had been on the market for two years. It was a great business, but the remote location put people off. I shared some insights on manifesting, energies, and frequencies with her, and I knew QJH could help her.

I suggested we do our next three sessions using the QJH method. In our first session, she said that this was what she wanted to achieve.

Release: Anxiety around selling the business

Acquire: Calm, Peace, Wisdom

Understand: Why I don't feel good enough

Transform: More loving heart

Louise shared that the evidence she would have to prove the miracles occurring would be to 'Have no anxiety knowing the business will sell and be nicer to herself and people around her.'

We delved a little deeper into our pre-talk and discovered that she never felt enough and always had to prove herself. Hopefully, through hypnosis, she will learn why she feels like this and gain insight into how to heal from it.

Session 1

As I knew Louise well, I decided to take her straight into a relaxed trance state. I began with the chakra deepener, and when I could see she was relaxed. I invited her to visualize her 'Happy Safe Place' where her body and conscious mind could rest. She shared that she was lying down in a grassy meadow filled with red flowers; there was a blue sky, and it was warm. She felt connected to the earth and could smell the dirt. She felt happy and relaxed.

From there, I invited her higher consciousness to 'The Temple of Healing'.

Doorway One 'Louise Met Her Guide.'

The first doorway was behind a dark wooden door. Inside was a long table with an envelope. When opened, it had a message that said, "It's ok. You don't need to feel afraid." Louise then said she felt calmer. I asked her to look around the room to see what else might show itself. She saw a gold cup, like a chalice, that was filled with liquid/ water. She then felt the presence of someone; it was an old lady, her guide, called Doris. Louise asked her what the liquid was, and she said LIFE – Life is fluid. It is not meant to be structured; it moves, but there is no need to be afraid.

She then asked Louise to put her hand in the water, and as it moved across her hand and fingers, Doris said, "Whatever is happening is part of your journey, and you should take joy from it. Just laugh to have a more loving heart; do not be so serious. Things do not have to be as planned. Just laugh it off." At this point, Doris gradually disappeared.

Doorway 2- 'Louise Met Her Inner Child.'

I asked Louise if there was anything else in this room for her. As she looked around, she saw another wooden door. When entering, she saw big windows with lots of light, and as she looked out, she saw lots of people rushing around. She said everyone was so busy and they all felt sad because they were not feeling the water. She said she felt she was inside all of them. I then asked Louise to visualise 'her' colour of love and breathe it into her heart until it expands out to the people. As she breathed in 'red,' she said their clothes were changing from pastel colours to bright, and they began chatting and laughing. She also felt she had more energy in her now.

I then asked if there was anything else in the room. She could see an ornate gold mirror. I asked her to look in it, and she gasped. There was a beast with horns. I told her to look at the beast and ask who it was. It did not answer her, so I suggested she say some affirmations to it, like, I am Strong. She started saying, "I am Love, I am Wise, I am Smart," etc. The beast just stayed there, looking back at her. I then suggested she say, 'I am Enough'.

At that point, the beast changed into her as a little girl. She even recognized the dress she was wearing. She smiled at her, and I asked Louise to ask her if she had any messages. She said, "The flowers are love; when you see a red flower, you feel the love. The water will feed the flowers, and the more you laugh, the more you will love."

We asked little Louise what would make her happy. She said, "You are strong and that makes me happy, but mix it with love. Relax and be calm, feel the water." Little Louise then faded from the mirror.

We left that room and went back into the hallway, which was just a bright light. Louise could see no more doors and felt it was time to leave the hallway.

As we returned to her happy, safe place, she noticed the flowers were even brighter red and their scent stronger.

Session 2

Release: Anxiety for the future

Acquire: Calmer, trust

Understand: Why I always worry about money

Transform: Confidence that things will be ok

Doorway 1- Louise Met Her Husband's Higher Consciousness.

In this session, I relaxed Louise with a Sun Grounding/ Energy Healing deepener, and she chose the same Happy place as before. This time, as Louise reached The Temple of Healing, she opened the door and entered the Hallway of Answers, which was a bright white corridor.

Louise could not see any doors, so I told her to look up or further down the hallway. She then saw a red door up high with a ladder leading to it. The room was dark, but when her eyes adjusted, she saw a big statue of a pig in the center. It did not move or offer anything, so I asked Louise to put her hands on it. She felt so much 'new energy'. She then started to receive a message.

"Let things fall where they lie, do not put your spin on things. Keep driving the bus – just drive it, don't forward think ahead. Every day, you will see the next turn but don't take your hands off the wheel". At this point, Louise started to cry and said she felt for her husband and didn't want to sense his disappointment by saying she was "just driving the bus."

I asked her to invite her husband's Higher Consciousness to see what it says. It said, "He doesn't feel as much frustration as you; just give him love, and don't hold back. Feel the water, laugh, see the red flowers, and be open to his love."

The pig then started to disintegrate like pixels. Louise returned to the hallway.

I looked up the spiritual meaning after the session, and the word pig represents wealth, abundance, and strength (hence, piggy bank).

Doorway 2 – Love Is the Key.

Louise found an arched wooden door; she entered the room and saw a big clock, and the time was 10 10. As she looked at it, she heard, "Don't give up faith and hope, it is not 12 o'clock yet." She then started sharing that she felt so much pressure to sell the business as they had given themselves a deadline of 31ˢᵗ March. She had two potential buyers and realised that her desperation and scarcity could push them away. She then noticed that there was a heart-shaped key in the center of the clock, representing love.

She stood there looking at it and then felt a presence with big wings holding her. It had a message, "Now you are exhausted, so just rest, and be open to love, joy, and laughter."

We left that room and dropped back down to her happy, safe place, where I decided to invite her future self at the end, as we have worked with her in the past with impressive results. I wanted to finish the session on an empowering note. Louise's future-self repeated that she holds the key, and it is in her heart, so open it up and let it shine.

Session 3

Release: Insomnia

Acquire: Relaxed attitude towards sleep

Understand: Why I keep waking up

Transform: Sleep through the night

Evidence of a miracle occurring. Feeling rested and energized in the morning.

With this session, I did not take Louise to the Hallway of Answers. I felt it was more appropriate to talk to the part of Louise that was preventing her from sleeping. I asked her to call upon that part and ask if it had a name. It said it did not have a name, so she then asked what its job was.

It was said to stop her from forgetting important things and help her get stuff done. We then asked if it could find other ways to help so that both it and Louise would feel more relaxed.

The part said that to have more order in life, space and calm are needed. We asked how that could happen, and it said to clean up the bedroom, have cool sheets, and put the phone away.

We then asked what we could give this part to help it and what it needed. It is said not to be in pain, to take something for the pain. I asked Louise what it meant, and she said her shoulder hurts at night. We asked if there was anything else, and it said self-care and self-love, stop trying to be everything to everyone else. When I delved deeper into this, Louise said she always felt she had to prove herself above and beyond to feel loved, as her mother favoured her brothers much more when they were growing up. Her mother is currently in Palliative care and still shows this behaviour towards Louise.

We then asked the part of Louise that doesn't sleep if she nurtured her inner child if it would feel peaceful, and it said yes.

I then went on to bring Louise's inner child out and had a conversation about what she needed. She told me that she wanted to be heard and loved. Louise told her she would do that, and we integrated 'Little Louise' into Louise's heart. She said her chest felt full and warm after.

We then went back to the original part and asked if there was anything else it needed or a message it wanted to share. It said that when you realise you are enough, you will sleep. Don't chase me, just invite me.

I finished the session by reprogramming Louise's subconscious mind so that when she gets into bed, she takes herself to her Happy Safe Place, and once she feels relaxed, sleep will come to her easily.

Results: In the last three months of working together and bringing QJH into our sessions, Louise has attracted two potential buyers. As of today, the sale hasn't yet gone through, but her attitude towards it has changed considerably. She has let go of the anxiety, still taking necessary action, and she now believes that what is meant to be will be. This is a vastly different attitude from when we first met. Her confidence has expanded, her relationships have blossomed, particularly her relationship with herself, and she is sleeping better.

I loved adding QJH to my toolbox. It was like the missing link that brought it all together.

> *It just delights me to see how different practitioners with different skills and talents weave their sessions together into a beautiful tapestry and healing. Lisa is incredibly gifted in many modalities and also extraordinarily intuitive, but as you can see, she uses her intuition only to formulate better questions for her clients rather than just telling them what she picks up. This is so much more empowering for our clients. To hear their own voice telling them what they most need to heal, transform, understand, or release is so much more powerful than just having someone tell you what they think.*
>
> *~Kryssa*

Aurora

By Persis Balsara-Wetzel

This case is about a client who wanted to relieve pain in the right side of her hip near the womb and bloating. She wanted to acquire peace, be pain-free, and move her body easily. She wanted to have a better understanding of her body and was curious as to where the pain was coming from. She said she would feel transformed when she felt lighter and danced without feeling any pain. She would know this transformation had taken place when she could dance the chakra dance easily and effortlessly.

The client went into a state of hypnosis beautifully and easily. She described her hallway of answers as a long, floating cloud with doorways on either side of the cloud. The doorways were described as little puffs of clouds with handles on them. There, she was met by her Higher Consciousness. She was tall and beautiful, with white hair, and she was wearing white clothes and jewels. She looked like light. She gave her name as Aurora, and she said she felt like a distant family member.

Behind her, she saw a group of other higher beings who felt like they were her ancestors, just present there and communicating with her in light language.

The client felt as though she knew this language; she didn't know what they were saying per se, but she felt it was very familiar. Aurora guided her through one of the doors into the Healing Temple. The healing temple was large and looked like a Roman church with huge pillars in the front. Everything was white.

When asking the client if she saw her inner healer, she mentioned that it was Aurora. Aurora was a part of her Consciousness that is the Inner Healer. She also saw her ancestors there.

Aurora then started scanning her body and found blockages in her throat and found that the right side of her hip near the womb and her ankle were holding on to trauma. Quickly, Aurora released the trauma and the blockages in all the affected parts and healed them. Aurora also did the emotional and spiritual healing.

In the Temple of Healing, the client could also feel the presence of Christ, besides the group of light beings, her ancestors, who said to her that they chose this time and space to come to inform her that it was all happening as it should.

Suddenly, Christ started giving her a message. He said that the message was for all present who were listening. "Everything is happening right now as it is meant to happen, no matter how hard it is. Everything will turn out well, and do not lose hope.

You all have important work for humanity: to raise your frequency and share your light. Do not let fear and ego get in the way. The Universe will always back you up to keep your light shining. Energy on Earth has tilted, but you should not allow that to affect you. Just let it slide off and continue to do the work."

After that, the client bid goodbye to her ancestors, and Aurora led her out to the Hallway of Answers. She then chose to go through another door, which turned out to be a banquet room.

There, the client was asked to do a water fast for a minimum of 2 days and then add more and more days if possible. She needed to do this to keep a clean channel and remove the toxins. The table had more fruits and vegetables, watermelon, oranges, peas, spinach, fish, and a little bit of cheese.

Once again, the client was led back out to the hallway, and she chose not to go through any more doors today. She bid Aurora goodbye and gave her a big hug, and when she hugged her, she felt as though she was hugging a close ancestor.

Before she returned from the hallway of answers, she was taken through the shower of light, where she experienced a beautiful, cleansing shower filled with unconditional love and protection.

On returning, the client felt that she had released her pain from the right side of her hip, and she had gained a higher perspective of the things she needed to do to be a clear channel. She was able to release the blocks in her throat and ankle and visualised herself dancing her chakra dance easily and effortlessly.

She was very humbled by the message from Christ, telling all those who were listening that everything was exactly as it was meant to be, and to be a beacon of light for the people and to keep sharing it.

I, as a hypnotist, thanked the client for a wonderful session and took her safely back to her happy, safe place and emerged.

Christ Consciousness, various Archangels, God/Source/All-That-Is, along with various Ascended Masters, ancestors, higher dimensional beings, other guides and helpers, are a very regular occurrence in QJH. I find this extremely interesting, given that I considered myself Agnostic -with a capital A- when I first ventured into hypnotherapy and hypnosis.

I say Agnostic -with a capital A- because I believed in something based on the two Near Death Experiences I'd had (though I still don't recall very much from the second one). However, there has never been any particular religion that felt like it fit the proverbial bill for me. And I tried! I not only attended different churches, preferring to stick with non-denominational if Christian-based, or non-Christian altogether, but nothing really fit.

I was raised with spirituality, but in a vague DIY sense, which I briefly rebelled against before making my way back. My mother converted to Judaism some years ago. She also studied Buddhism many years ago. But she never imposed any of her beliefs upon me- with the possible exception of Astrology, which I'm still on the fence about if I'm honest.

This allows me to accept my clients' beliefs with objectivity, and not feel the need to impose my own on them, or interpret theirs for them, or contradict them because they don't match up with mine. I request that 2JHA students do their very best to take a similar objective stance, at least when dealing with clients and facilitating sessions.

I have learned that I am equal parts logical and intuitive, which is GREAT for making decisions and determining life path type stuff, as well as just trusting myself and my experiences, but not so great for coming to any sort of firm acceptance of proscribed religious or spiritual paradigms. Maybe my karma ran over my dogma in another life...just kidding. Sorry, I couldn't resist.

But in all seriousness, I have very few "beliefs" that I would stand firm on, and if presented with opposing, compelling evidence, I believe I would still remain open to changing them.

Well, all except for one. And that one is that we're all on different parts of our journey, and while we each have very individual, very personal reasons for doing whatever we're doing in this life (most of which we aren't even consciously aware of), I do now believe there is a singularity of consciousness that runs through all of us. Not just us humans, but every atom. Every particle. I've witnessed this. I've communicated with it. (I believe you have too, even if you were unaware of it at the time). And one day, I believe we will accept this as truth.

~Kryssa

Faith, Fatherhood, and Frequency

By Shelley Whisler

Carlos A. contacted me looking for help with physical healing through a Quantum Journeys Hypnosis session.

His once robust life as a husband, father, and successful businessman and teacher had been unraveled due to a mysterious illness that was like Parkinson's disease. It was linked to the body's inability to produce dopamine, causing a movement disorder and great physical pain.

I watched as he struggled up the few stairs to meet with me for our first session. He shared with me the distress of no longer being able to walk well or take his wife dancing or work and be the provider for his family that he once was. He missed playing ball with his son, jogging with his daughter, and dancing with his wife. His dream of becoming a university professor seemed all but lost. Pain and frustration clouded his once joy-filled life.

Carlos was and is a man of great faith. His approach to his healing was to include everything his doctors and priests could offer and to bring in additional healing modalities. His strong desire and faith to become whole and healthy again opened many doors of possibility to achieve complete healing.

I admired his faith and perseverance and respected the strength and hope his religion provided. As a healer and a Quantum Journeys Hypnosis practitioner, I know it is imperative to join the client in their model of the world. This can include their religion or spiritual path as well as a belief system, values, and any perceived blockages or limitations to full health and healing on all levels. I know we are unlimited spiritual beings in a physical body and have many challenging experiences on this earthly plane.

We began our session with a conversation so I could better understand what Carlos wished to receive from our sessions and what he ultimately wanted to experience in his life. He desired complete wellness, recovery, and restoration of full health and healing. He wanted his joy back. He wanted to be able to dance again with his wife and to shake his booty! He longed to be the provider for his family again, and he very much wanted a new, meaningful path in his career when his health was restored. Prior to his illness, he had been striving for 10 long years to become a tenured professor at a local university. This was his dream job and would provide him with great fulfillment and security for his family. He wanted to embody and manifest the best version of himself in this lifetime.

Carlos's healing team included medical doctors, his Priests, Reiki Masters, Sound Healers, and me. His medical doctors offered some allopathic treatments but were unsure of their efficacy, so those treatments also relied on Carlos's faith that they would be beneficial. His faith was the healing thread and Guiding Light that connected all that he was doing.

After making sure Carlos was physically comfortable and that his conscious, analytical mind or present consciousness was resting comfortably, we were able to begin. Expanding his Consciousness through the QJH protocols, we traveled through the Subconscious mind to the Higher Consciousness and Interdimensional Consciousness, which holds the wisdom, guidance, and healing of our interdimensional being.

We entered the Hallway of Answers, and Carlos was guided to select a doorway from many, which led him to the Temple of Healing. There, he met his Inner Healer, whose name was Joe. Joe assisted Carlos in evaluating and selecting the best foods and supplements for his body. We were also joined in the quantum consciousness by Carlos Sr., who is Carlos's father and is still living. (To draw upon Quantum Physics, this is an example of non-locality and entanglement. Everything and everyone that has been connected stays connected. In the quantum field, we are not limited by time and space. Our consciousness can join or be joined by others as we experience our dreamtime, meditations, or other forms of journeying.) Joe and Carlos Sr. were asked to scan Carlos's body for anything that needed attention and healing.

Pain was present in the right shoulder, and I instructed Carlos on how to utilize the Control Room of his mind to turn the dial down on that pain. He experienced immediate relief. He was also guided on how to turn the dial up on his ability to create and release much-needed dopamine. The strong message he received from Carlos Sr was not to have any doubt about his ability to heal. He must utilize his strong faith and never allow doubt to enter into his healing journey. I confirmed that he believed he could have full healing in his body, making sure there were no doubts or limiting beliefs that might impede his progress.

Many colors and sensations were noticed throughout the body. The best colors for healing, as shared by Carlos, were utilized as well. Every part of the body, down to the cells, atoms, and DNA, was infused with healing colors and helpful emotions. A warm golden healing light flowed down from the top of his head through the body to encode every cell with strength and healing. The cells were called to remember and embrace the feelings of freedom, movement, dancing, running, and walking with ease. The cells are always listening for direction and were reminded to open with complete gratitude to accept Divine Healing. Reminders were installed to make this happen on an ongoing basis.

I thanked Joe and Carlos Sr for joining us and helping in Carlos's healing process. I guided Carlos's highest consciousness back to the Hallway of Answers. Many doorways were presented that could lead to a past life, a time between lifetimes, or the Akashic records, to name a few. I instructed Carlos to stand at the doorway that would be for his highest good and benefit to enter today.

Carlos stood before a red door, placed his hand on a metal handle, and opened the door. He entered a room with a table, a chair, and a bookshelf. He was drawn to a particular book on the shelf, and he went over to take a closer look. The book had a beautiful peach-colored cover, and the edges of the pages were gold-colored leaves.

Always leaving the choices up to the client, I asked Carlos what he would like to do with the book. He decided to take the book over to the table, sat down in the chair, and opened the book. The Book took a Holographic form, and he noticed the first page was blank. Carlos knew that this was his book of life and that it was for him to write his future.

Giving him ample time to notice all that was around him, angels soon appear and remind him that we create our experiences, so now it's time to create the future he wants. He was able to write in his book of life through his vision and feelings of full health and healing. As he turns the pages of this holographic book, he sees himself dancing with his wife, laughing, and shaking his booty!

This vision becomes a creation in the quantum realm. Holographic healing sends and receives vibrational healing into the body across time and space. And we don't know, on the physical level, if this will be in a month or a year or five years, but the joy of embracing the new reality and having faith that it is so are carried forward in time. The timeline is sped up with the

Quantum Jump instructions to Carlos to collapse time and speed healing to hasten his desired future.

Much gratitude was given to Carlos's highest consciousness for all that had taken place. Reminders were anchored in the fact that the vibrational waves of healing from the holographic universe are ongoing and respond to our thoughts and feelings.

Carlos was then integrated back into his conscious mind and body. Suggestions were made to keep a gratitude journal to remember his vision of being healed and restored, as it is now written in his book of life. Our future is not separate from today, but it is entangled with the Oneness of all energy, which we create daily.

A few months later, I received a message from Carlos thanking me for my help, healing work, and faith in his recovery. His progress was going well.

A year later, I was pleasantly surprised to see Carlos at a community gathering. I was amazed to see such a healthy, strong man standing before me. The physical transformation was remarkable. He was beaming with joy, vitality, and gratitude for life. His family is doing well, and he is back to his previous activities. He also shared, a miracle of miracles, that he had not only returned to work but had also landed his dream job, and it is going wonderfully. He is thriving and healthy, dancing with his wife and even shaking his booty.

This is a perfect example of the concept of communicating with multidimensional consciousness through the idea of a singularity of consciousness. Carlos was communicating with the cells of his physical body while also communicating with the higher consciousness of his father, all through a conversation with an aspect of his own consciousness that has access to both and all.

Doing this work benefits our clients on multiple levels, layers, densities, and dimensions. It's not only helpful in the practical sense of physical health and landing dream jobs, but also in manifesting abundance, etc. And it's also not just about exploring other lifetimes or meeting our unseen guides and helpers, renegotiating agreements in the Akashic records, etc.

We aren't split up into distinctly separate pieces of consciousness, and therefore our lives aren't only this and not that. We can only perceive the dimension just below us. Just like a one-dimensional dot doesn't realize it's a one-dimensional dot until it can see itself from the second dimension. And a two-dimensional line can't perceive itself as two-dimensional until it can see itself from the third dimension. And we humans cannot perceive ourselves as three-dimensional unless we're doing so from the fourth dimension, which is time. What aspects of ourselves are being perceived by us from the fifth dimension? Sixth? And so on. Just because our current conscious understanding is in the fourth dimension, perceiving ourselves in the third dimension doesn't mean that's all that we are.

~Kryssa

Finding Inner Strength

By Nikki Hoare

Sarah (not her real name) came in to see me as she wanted her energy and strength back. There have been a lot of bad things that have seemed to happen over time, especially over the last year, to the females in her family, and she wanted to have the strength to help them. She told me how she had six miscarriages, and her daughter also lost a baby recently. Her mum has cancer, and their dog was very ill.

When I asked her what she wanted, her response was, "To find answers to why I'm having bad luck at the moment. Also, why are females in my family having bad health, including our dog (bitch), and I'm losing twins? Is something bigger playing out?"

Sarah's response to the RAUT questions was to release any attachments, acquire happiness for her family, and understand her purpose on this planet. She was not sure what she wanted to transform about herself.

After getting her agreement that she was ready to go into hypnosis and go on this amazing journey together, I explained what we would be doing and then went through it with her, guiding her along the way.

Following the induction and deepener, I guided Sarah to her peaceful place, but when I asked her to describe what she could sense, see, feel, or know of this place, she was silent for a while. She then said, "I am not there yet. I feel like there was something drawing me, something I had to do. I am at the top of a mountain. The sky is beautiful, and the clouds are blue and white. I notice now my babies are here with me, my beautiful babies. The ones that I lost."

(She had a small tear roll down her face, but she was smiling)

After a short while, she continued, "They are speaking to me. They tell me not to be sad, not to worry. It was not their time, but that is alright. It is time for them to go now. I see them. They are getting their wings. I want to go with them, to care for them, but they tell me it is not my time. I have others who need me right now. They will be there and see me at the end."

(More tears started to roll down Sarah's face as she took a deep breath)

I gave her time to let go, and when she seemed calm and ready to continue, I asked if she was ready.

"Yes," she replied.

She went down deeper into her happy, safe place. When she was ready, I asked her to describe what she could sense, see, feel, or know about where she was.

"I am by a river; it is warm and calm. I feel happy and relaxed here."

When asked to find somewhere for her conscious mind to sleep for a while, she said there was a boat tied up at the side. Settling down in the boat, allowing the rocking to take her deeper, we continued up to the hallway of answers.

When Sarah stepped through the doorway, though she was not in a hallway, she found herself again at the top of a mountain. She felt that she was not alone here. There was a presence around her. I asked if she wanted to speak to that presence and find out who or what they were. "It is my highest wisdom; she is called Ana. I suggested that she thank Ana for coming to speak with her and ask her what she wanted to know. Sarah asked Ana why she was having all the bad luck and if there was something she had to understand.

Ana responded, "It was part of your contract. You had to learn these things and experience those times to better understand."

Sarah asked, "Do I have more to learn?"

Ana replied, "No, that contract is now complete and has been burned."

Sarah then said, "But I love my family and do not want them to suffer. How can I help them?"

"Ana says nothing but has given me a candle, a yellow candle."

Sarah then described going around a house, filling the house with healing light. Shining it across various areas.

"Ah, I understand now. I am not responsible for their health, but how can I help them? How do I get the strength to be there for them?"

After a moment, Sarah said, "The scene is changing, I see myself as a man. There is nothing much around me. I have bear feet, and there is material tied around my waist. My arms ache, and I am hurt. I can now see some men below me wearing helmets. They are reaching up to me, lifting me down. My body is dirty, and there is blood and sweat. I feel so tired. They are lying me down now in some dark place and leaving, closing the doorway."

Sarah then said, "I don't get it. Why are you showing me this?"

"Now I am a man, one of the Marvel characters that is one in blue. I think...is that Captain America?"

"I am now standing by a river next to a large stone. In the stone, there is a sword, and someone is pulling at it, but it doesn't move. They are beckoning me over to pull at it, and it comes out."

"It's becoming cold. Things are changing again. There is snow and ice everywhere, and lots of people are around. I am in a blue and white floaty dress, and coldness is coming out of my hands. There is a metal ball in the corner of the room. No, it is a barrier – I am strong, and you cannot stop me. Oh, bloody hell, I am Elsa. What is this all about?"

"Oh, I am back on the mountain now with my highest wisdom. I don't understand. What are you showing me?"

Sarah went quiet for a while, and then she said, "Ana is telling me I asked for strength, but I already have it. Oh, I get it now. I was not each of them. They are symbols of strength in me. I am already strong enough, and I just need to believe in myself more. Ana is now showing me a golden ring with a ruby. It was my mum's ring. She is telling me to wear this more so that I feel connected and strong. Take care of myself more and find the time to go to the gym.

When I am healthy and well, I will have more energy to be there for others."

Sarah takes a deep breath and smiles. I asked her if there was anything else she needed to do or know.

"No, it's all done now. I have my ring."

I asked her to place her hands over her heart and take a deep breath, and as you do, you could install all the knowledge and all the learnings from this visit today, bringing them back with you to the here and now. Letting go of any negative feelings and releasing any stress. When you are ready, you can drift back down to your conscious self, resting there in that boat by the river.

I then continued to bring Sarah back to the here and now, bringing all that learning and knowledge with her. When she opened her eyes, she took a moment and then started to smile, "Oh my goodness, that was something else. I get it now. I have the strength I need, and by taking better care of myself, I will be able to cope better. I am going to wear my mother's ring every day."

About ten months later, Sarah messaged me to say that things had picked up. Her mum's cancer was in remission. Her daughter had a baby boy, and both are happy and healthy. Sarah herself was feeling fantastic, she is now working at a centre helping people, and she enjoys going swimming and a dance class each week.

Clients often come to us with questions like, "Why is this happening to me?", "Am I being punished?", "Is this bad luck to pay for past sins?" and other similar inquiries.

More often than not, once they receive communication from their higher consciousness, they are told that this was all part of the plan or that if it wasn't, it will still be okay because there are many gifts that come with loss, grief, a sense of betrayal, and going through what some call "the dark night of the soul".

Having had the always unexpected, but greatly appreciated, good fortune to tap into higher collective consciousness both on my own as well as during client sessions, I've been able to ask about these kinds of existential pain and its purpose- and receive responses.

From our 3D human perspective, these kinds of events seem like punishment. That bad things wouldn't happen to good people, therefore, if bad things happen, one must be a bad person. Sadly, I even see many spiritually minded people fall for this. And the flip side, which is even more toxic (and at the heart of most cult-like, con artist guru philosophies), is that success and prosperity and abundance only happen to good people. And I have it on pretty good authority that this is not at all the case.

From the perspective of our higher consciousness, which lives in a realm that doesn't have access to painful emotions like sadness, grief, loss, heartbreak, betrayal, etc., experiencing these things is considered brave and beautiful and almost delicious. They are flavors that cannot be experienced any other way.

Or, to use another metaphor, imagine that you are playing a video game, and you have the option of playing a character that has a stable but bland and boring life. No major challenges to overcome and gain confidence, no obstacles to learn how to clear and gain resilience, no frightening experiences to teach them about fear…just wake up and have enough money for everything and delicious food and a content life with safe people who all care about you and go to bed and sleep well and wake up and do it all over again. OR, you have the option of playing a character who has many challenges and obstacles and frightening experiences, and every day they learn more and more about themselves while developing tools and talents that they would never have unearthed if not for the hardships they survived. Which character would you choose?

Chances are, if you're anything like me, you immediately think to yourself, "Of course I'd choose the easy life. Who wouldn't?"

But ponder it a bit more. Who would you be today without the challenges you've already successfully survived? You for sure wouldn't be the you that is reading this book! This book would hold absolutely no interest for you. Or, if it did, it wouldn't make any sense. You'd have no foundation through which to empathize with these stories.

So, while it is human nature to mistake bad things as punishment and good things as rewards, at the higher levels of our consciousness, this isn't so. And it's not that our higher selves want to keep us in perpetual pain or anything…the point is to continue to grow and expand our awareness of ourselves and discover new strengths and wisdom.

The ideal here is that we learn to hold love within us as we move through hardships, realizing that hardships are really just neutral experiences that we give painful meanings to. If we can allow them to be neutral, as we continue to hold love and point ourselves in the direction of joy even under the harshest of circumstances, then we've upleveled to the point where there is no hardship. There are only neutral experiences, and we are always loved.

When we perceive the joy in every experience, our experiences begin to reflect that joy back to us. That is, I believe, the true meaning of "We create our own reality.

~Kryssa

Channeling the "I Am"

By Cassidy Green

As a QJ Hypnotist, I have the privilege of guiding individuals through transformative journeys, unraveling the depths of their subconscious minds.

One such remarkable individual, Sean, a high-powered executive burdened by the weight of burnout and the fear of change, sought my expertise to explore a new path.

In our initial session, we delved into parts of the work, unraveling the depth of fear that had embedded itself within the very makeup of his being. To Sean's surprise, we unearthed a fragment of his consciousness with a name - Sly, a trace of a childhood incident when fear took root when he was young, and a father's misguided attempt to dispel it by using vulgar language when Sean was too afraid to go down the tall slide.

Sly, once a harbinger of fear that would keep Sean trapped and not embrace change, was now promoted from Fear to the role of Farmer, sowing the seeds of fresh ideas and beliefs. Sly changed his name from Sly to Atlas, exuding excitement in his overalls and straw hat.

Sean then went to an ethereal, white, otherworldly space. Within this meaningful space, he encountered his Highest-Self, known in this case as "I Am," who guided him to a magnificent circular room adorned with a podium bearing a mysterious, boundless book. A monumental being cloaked in gray materialized, prompting an offering, which, in a profound twist, manifested as the seeds left by Sly. As Sean stood before the mysterious book, his hands hovering over its wordless pages, an influx of knowledge rushed forth, and a profound exchange between "I Am," the book, and his receptive consciousness.

The revelations that permeated his being at that moment within the Akashic records altered the trajectory of his life, infusing him with newfound purpose and clarity.

Sean plans to leave his executive career and start a non-profit, no-till-producing farm where he will employ adults with Down syndrome and autism.

> *Ah, yes, the "I Am". If you've been in the world of New Age concepts, spirituality, and/or the metaphysical for any length of*

time, you've likely run into this aspect of our higher consciousness known simply as "I Am".

I don't know any more than anyone else about this mysterious part of us, except to say that it seems to have the ability to bridge communication between ALL aspects of us, right on up to Source or God or Creator, or whatever other word you may use for the idea of the original singularity of consciousness that may have created all of…everything. I suspect that we're dealing with the "I Am" far more frequently than we're aware of, but it doesn't always refer to itself that way. My guess is that it shows up as whatever we most need in the moment, like an avatar of sorts.

If you're fortunate enough to channel this aspect of your consciousness, ask all the questions you can think of because it certainly seems to know just about everything.

~Kryssa

Yearning For More

By Cassidy Green

Clara came to me because she was feeling stuck in her life. She stated her life was filled with blessings: a successful husband, a thriving daughter, and a cherished small business. Yet, she yearned to contribute more to her family's financial well-being without compromising the unique essence of her special offering.

Uncertain of the path to pursue, Clara was ready to embark on a Quantum Journey Hypnosis (QJH) session to unlock the answers that lay dormant within her.

As Clara and I traveled to the Hallway of Answers, its beauty unfolded before her. Intricate pillars adorned the space, reaching up to expose the open expanse of the universe above. The floor was decorated with black and white marble tiles, emitting warmth beneath Clara's bare feet.

Each door, crafted from thick mahogany, stood tall and arched. Their glass doorknobs became beautiful fractals or rainbow colors the closer she looked.

Amidst this beautiful space, Clara's highest-self emerged, introducing herself as Ariel.

Guided by Ariel, Clara stepped through a wooden door into a room enveloped in cascading wooden paneling. Bookshelves lined the walls, with ladders and a seemingly infinite wooden spiral staircase at its center. A luxurious purple velvet couch called Clara to sit, and as she did, Ariel instructed her to open a specific book. With the book in hand, the bookcase shifted and revealed a hidden room where a majestic, larger-than-life book awaited.

As Clara approached the special book, she found herself speechless, her hands suspended in mid-air, unable to articulate her thoughts. Sensing Clara's struggle, Ariel guided her toward another room known as the Knowing Room. Clara described this space as reminiscent of Roman architecture, adorned with lush greenery.

In front of her was a stone table that she climbed up onto and lay herself down upon, surrounded by additional guides who began infusing her with vivid imagery. At first, Clara's voice came through in a language I could not understand, but the guides adapted, allowing the profound message to be in English. However, she now had a different accent.

The voice resonated, affirming Clara's true essence as God's lion, urging her to embrace her inner strength and cease hiding. It implored her to cast aside concerns of others' opinions, for in doing so, she confined herself to a smaller existence. Clara was not small but mighty, and the world awaited the resonance of her voice, a voice that could only be heard when she played on a grander stage. Clara's guides had her step into the shower of light, her face radiating a newfound glow.

Encouraged by the revelations she received, Clara embarked on a transformative journey. She began group coaching, intertwining her unique gift within a VIP coaching program, no longer content to play it small.

I'm so glad one of these client session stories includes the concept of using our natural, or authentic, voice resonance. This is something that has come up in my own meditations many times, with emphasis to pass it along to my students and anyone else willing to hear of it.

The idea is this: Each of us has the ability to provide healing to our own body through the sound frequencies of our natural voice resonance and tones. We are perfectly calibrated to provide this for ourselves in the form of chanting and humming, much like cats and their purring. Our natural voice tone and resonance are also like a sound frequency calling card, with magnetic properties. It will draw certain people to us while repelling others. I've lost count of how many people have reached out to me either for sessions or training after hearing me on a podcast or seeing me in a YouTube or TikTok video or Instagram reel. Our voices are powerful instruments!

Unfortunately, many women in cultures across the planet are praised and rewarded for continuing to sound like demure, submissive little girls well into adulthood. This higher-pitched, false tone and resonance aren't doing their bodies any favors as they're missing out on the natural healing properties of their authentic tones…and it's also not attracting their 'tribe' to them. Instead, it's likely attracting people who desire false dominance.

~Kryssa

Breaking Free from Shackles and Soul Contracts

By Carolyn Mather

The client wanted to release feelings of low self-worth, the need to force herself to be happy, and the need to comfort eat with chocolate. She wanted to acquire a feeling of self-worth and self-love, the ability to be naturally happy, and to understand why she had always felt different from others (this was just curiosity—she didn't necessarily want to change this). Most of all, she wanted to transform so that she could recognize her self-worth and not have to force herself to try to be happy, but instead to feel more connected.

I have completed Angelic Reiki training and discovered that this blends wonderfully with QJH. I set up the space prior to the session, asked for the most perfect angel to join us, and requested that guidance and angelic healing energy be channeled during the session. When merging with the client's energy and the angel, I sensed a golden light around the client, which felt like a sixth sense. I could also feel angels all around us.

The client's safe, happy place was a beautiful beach in the sun. The hallway was pure white light; there were no windows or doors, and it wasn't clear whether it was day or night. The client simply went through a portal to where she needed to be, which was a wooden house. The client's higher-self, "Mary," was already there with her, standing by her side. We asked Mary if she was able to help with the client's goals, and she said yes. When asked what needed to be done, Mary told us the answer was in a past life and that the client needed to see it herself to understand. I asked Mary to take us there, but we realized we were already there.

The client described a little wooden house, like a shack, in a small village with dry soil floors, where she was a young woman. She spoke of seeing people walking past in groups, looking at her as if she were a complete outsider. She was always trying to do her best, but no matter what she tried, it made no difference. She felt completely worthless. It was Connecticut in the 1800s. The name of the woman wouldn't come, but her higher-self told her she didn't need to know the name.

Her husband was very abusive. He was cruel and always putting her down, constantly telling her she was doing things wrong. From a bird's-eye view, and with Mary's guidance, she was able to see that she had done nothing wrong. She had always tried so hard, and it was not her fault. People just stood by and watched while she was abused—they did nothing. She always felt worthless.

She had been strangled to death by her husband in front of her two children, ages four and five. The client felt that those children were also her children in this lifetime. The husband may have been her ex-partner in this life, but she wasn't sure. Perhaps he simply represented many ex-partners from the same pattern that had repeated over and over.

Watching this from above, the client saw and felt the anger of her husband as he took her life. I asked for the young woman to be allowed to gently and peacefully drift up, back to Source, back to the light, reintegrating with the rest of the soul, becoming fully healed and whole, and taking on the wisdom that she had done nothing wrong. After the session, the client explained that she had seen an afterlife presence, where she was earthbound for a while following her death, watching her children. She had been filled with sorrow and a feeling of helplessness.

We allowed this lifetime to gently fade and asked Mary if anything else needed to be done. She said she needed to remove blocks. It took some time and was difficult, but Mary confirmed she didn't need any help. When the block was finally removed, the client said she felt the shackles break off and that an ancestral curse and soul contract had been broken.

This part was done in silence during the session. Afterwards, the client explained that she had seen the contract being ripped up. A demon tried to stop this, but the angels came in forcefully to prevent it. It wasn't easy; there were forces that didn't want the contract broken.

They didn't want to let go. She saw the paper contract—an old scroll—being torn up. It was released with anger and force, then burned in a fire. A demon devil came out of the flames, broke free from its chain, and went up in black smoke through a portal in the sky. Mary said it was "done." The client saw shackles breaking off, and she had broken free. Mary said there was nothing else to do "for now."

The client and Mary walked back to the hallway, which was still brightly lit. The client reported that it was like The Matrix—seeing loads of numbers, lightbulbs sparking off in her brain, and receiving multiple downloads. She felt things unlocking and swooshing, felt herself being pulled up and spun, and sensed changes occurring across multiple generations. She watched the town around her changing, felt an energy shift, a full upgrade, and a transformation within herself. She had always felt a suppressed feeling, a disconnect with people, as if things never flowed. Although she had always gotten on with people, it had been at a distance, with something pressing down in the background. She watched that energy block shift and felt things being upgraded.

Mary gave her a message: "You are free, my child." She agreed to increase the percentage of connection with her and suggested that the client journal about her feelings.

Following the session, the client realized that the lifetime we had visited was linked to all her feelings of low self-worth and her relationships. The same pattern had been repeating, with breakups always happening when her children were the same age as they are now—and as they were in that previous life. She could see how this had impacted her life. She had always felt as though something were pressing on her and suppressing her when talking to people, but she no longer felt the sadness. She felt the block had been lifted. She is no longer suppressed. She is free.

There are moments in hypnosis sessions when I feel like I'm watching history untangle itself—not the history in our textbooks, but the history written into our cells, our subconscious patterns, and our energy fields. This story is one of those moments.

We often talk about "ancestral trauma" in psychology and healing circles, but in hypnosis, it doesn't just remain a metaphor. It shows up vividly—sometimes as past lives, sometimes as symbolic imagery, sometimes even as these eerie, almost cinematic scrolls or contracts that clients perceive. Whether we interpret these as literal past lives or as subconscious archetypes doesn't matter as much as the fact that when the subconscious shows them, it is revealing something important about the repeating cycles that have been running the show.

I'm particularly struck by how the client here described the sameness of the pattern—worthlessness, suppression, abusive relationships, even the repeated ages at which her children mirrored those old traumas. This is what Jung might call the "complex" or what neuroscientists might label a "deeply encoded network," but the experience in trance makes it visceral. You can feel the weight of the shackles, and you can see the contract being ripped apart. It's as if the subconscious finally declares: enough.

And let's talk about those forces that "didn't want to let go." Anyone who has worked with subconscious sabotage, addictions, or even just a stubborn inner critic knows this energy. It can feel like demons, shadows, blocks— whatever language resonates. To me, it's often the parts of us that have been trying to keep us safe in outdated ways. They cling because they don't yet realize there's a new job available, one that doesn't involve pain or limitation.

When the client described downloads, spinning, upgrades, and the imagery of The Matrix, I couldn't help but smile. This is such a beautiful reflection of what I call the re-patterning moment. The subconscious doesn't just delete the old program; it installs a new one. These experiences can feel electric, dizzying, or like a sudden rush of clarity— but the after-effect is often unmistakable lightness, freedom, and expansion.

I also love that the higher-self's final message was so simple: "You are free, my child." After years—lifetimes, really—of suppression and false narratives, freedom doesn't come in the form of a complicated philosophical teaching. It comes in the form of a truth so simple the heart immediately recognizes it.

What I take from this story is the reminder that healing isn't just about easing symptoms—it's about breaking contracts, whether ancestral, energetic, or psychological, that were never meant to define us in the first place. Hypnosis gives us the opportunity to witness those contracts in whatever form they take, and then finally, lovingly, tear them up.

~Kryssa

Angels and Loved Ones

By Carolyn Mather

The client was hoping to release anxiety, gain more control over their eating habits, and lose unwanted weight. This was session three. During previous sessions, their higher-self had helped them release fear and pain, put down baggage they had been carrying around relating to negative things other people had said to them, filled them up with light, and "stretched them out" to make them longer and taller. The client had changed their eating habits with incredible ease after the first session and had experienced fantastic weight loss. However, doubt then crept in, and they began to self-sabotage.

During this session, we spoke to the party that was responsible for the sabotage. The part's name was Anger, and it looked like the client. The part explained that it had been there since the client was nine years old, after the client had written a poem and shown it to a family member, who gave a negative reaction. The part came in at that time, and its job was to protect the client by preventing them from trying anything new, believing they "would only fail anyway." The part was thanked for doing this very important job and reassured that it was not being reprimanded, but rather offered a promotion. We suggested a new role, and it said it was willing to try. When asked what it needed, it replied with love and forgiveness, which the client gave it. It agreed to protect the client from now on by being supportive of their goal to become healthier. It changed in appearance, becoming lighter.

During hypnosis, the client met with their higher-self in the hallway of answers. It was dark, with a red floor and old-fashioned torches lighting the way, and a big wooden door at the end. The client's higher-self said we needed to sit in the hallway and look at the door. I asked if any loved ones wanted to join us, and we were joined by their dad. I asked if he had any messages for the client. He said, "I miss you, I am always with you, you can do it, you are strong." The higher-self then said we needed to go through the wooden door to accomplish what needed to be done. We went through the door, and the higher-self got to work. They said the client needed to see the light, and that their higher-self was always there. The higher-self agreed to increase the client's connection with them and also with their dad, to make communication easier. They said the client would know when they were communicating with them, as they would feel the energy shift.

The higher-self filled the client with love, joy, good energy, and hope. The client said they could feel the good energy fizzing. When asked what else needed to be done, the higher-self explained they needed to remove a block. The block was linked to the family member who had given the negative reaction when the client was nine years old, and the block carried a lot of guilt. The higher-self said the block was difficult to remove because the family member's energy was so strong. I advised that they could call in help from anyone they needed. They called in St. Anthony and the angels of love and peace. The block began to dissolve, but it was still slow and difficult to remove. I asked the higher-self if they felt they could ask the family member's higher-self for a conversation, and they agreed to try. I said this could be done privately or shared, depending on their choice. The higher-self of the family member apologized, saying they hadn't meant to cause harm. They explained they had not known any other way to be, and that they had actually been in awe of the client's strength, almost jealous. They expressed genuine sorrow. The client was able to realize they no longer needed to carry the guilt, and the block finally dissolved.

We thanked the higher selves, the angels, and Dad. I asked for a final message from Dad, and he reassured the client that he was always with them and that they could achieve anything. I asked if anything else needed to be done. The client said they needed Dad to hold them—and he did.

The higher-self agreed to fully download, install, and activate the changes on all levels. They also explained that every time the client felt tempted to return to old habits, they would instead be filled with the healing light from earlier (referring to the beautiful golden light flowing through the body as part of the induction).

This session took place over Zoom. Changes in energy and shifts in the client are always visible, and part of any hypnosis session is observing these. But during this session, when the client's dad and the angels were present, I not only saw it—I felt it.

I never cease to be amazed by how often our so-called "negative parts" turn out to be protectors in disguise. In this client's case, the part named Anger wasn't sabotaging her for the sake of destruction—it was trying to keep her safe from failure, rejection, and pain. That's the paradox of these inner parts: they cling to outdated jobs, doing the best they know how, even if their methods hold us back.

What strikes me most here is the role of childhood wounding in shaping adult patterns. One poem, shown to a family member at nine years old, met with criticism instead of encouragement. And that moment planted a seed of self-protection that grew into decades of self-sabotage. Neuroscience would tell us that highly emotional childhood events encode strongly in the brain, creating networks that get reactivated again and again in adulthood. Hypnosis gives us the chance to revisit those moments—not to erase them, but to reframe them, and to release the protective strategies that no longer serve us.

And then there's the beautiful presence of the father. Grief often shows up as guilt or longing, but when loved ones appear in these sessions, the message is almost always the same: I'm still here, I'm still with you, and you're stronger than you know. Whether we think of this as the subconscious offering comfort in a familiar voice, or the genuine *presence of loved ones in spirit, the result is the same: the client feels seen, held, and supported. Sometimes that is the very thing that allows the block to dissolve.*

What I especially love about this session is how practical the higher-self was about the future. Every time the old habits try to creep back in, the client will instead be filled with the golden healing light. That's more than a metaphor—it's a rewiring. The subconscious now has a new job description, a new pathway to run, one that supports health and vitality instead of sabotage.

We often think of healing as this lofty, intangible process, but here we see its essence: releasing guilt, receiving forgiveness, and allowing love to take up residence where fear once lived. This is the work of hypnosis—not to overwrite the past, but to transform our relationship with it so that the present becomes lighter, freer, and more aligned with who we truly are.

~Kryssa

Part One: The Feather and the Fire

By Nikki Hoare

Emma (not her real name) had a previous QJH session with me, and this time was interested in visiting her Temple of Healing to see if she could meet her inner healer and gain some physical healing and inner peace.

When in trance, Emma did not go to her healing temple. Instead, after surrounding herself in a protective bubble, she found herself walking along a path in a forest. There was a presence—a small, impish chap standing on the path. He was called Hector, dressed in animal furs with a leaf hat. He was about the size of a child and carried a cane made from a branch.

Hector led Emma through the forest to a house, triangular in shape, covered in moss and ivy. The door was made from a tree trunk. (Emma physically held up her hand to touch it.) As she did, she told me that she was expected and that she should go inside.

Inside the house, she described what she could see: "Lots of candles, beautiful light everywhere, warm.

There is an old-fashioned bed covered in animal furs."

There was an old Aboriginal woman with grey hair, wearing animal furs. She was beautiful. Emma asked who she was. Her name was "Shanty," a healer.

Shanty guided Emma to lie down on the bed and began to move her hands over Emma, gently touching her chest, face, and head. (Emma indicated the places as she spoke by touching them with her own hands.)

Other women came into the room and stood around the bed. Emma said she felt like she was floating, a warm sensation like an energy pulsing through her body. Then Emma began to chant in another language. Her voice was quieter, softer, reaching her hands out wide as she chanted.

Then Emma said that Shanty and the other women were cleansing her—wrapping her with soil and herbs, sage and rosemary. "I know those smells," Emma said, wiping her own hands across her body as she spoke. She then started to tap out a beat on her leg, chanting again in the same foreign language as before.

After a short while, Emma became quiet and still. Then she said there was a knock at the door. Shanty opened it to find Hector standing there. Shanty turned and gave Emma a large feather before Emma left with Hector.

Emma said she understood now—she had been here before, a very long time ago. Another lifetime. This was her home. She was a Native American Indian—she could see it now. She had long dark hair, and she was dancing around a fire. "It's my wedding day, and I have a feather in my hair. It looks like the same feather I was given before."

There was a sense of community; children were playing and laughing. She continued to describe the village and the surroundings. They were by a river. The buildings were solid but could be packed up and moved.

Emma began to cry. "I am in my early twenties. There is a familiar feel to one particular tepee. Inside, there is a fire and pots. I reach out my hands as if to hug someone—Mama."

"I am home. My name is Gannowa. Mama is telling me to be at peace, that I can come back for healing anytime. Oh—I died in childbirth. That was a burial ritual—my burial. Mama shows me that my bones are with them. I will go with them always. I see my child.

She is beautiful, and they have called her Gannowa after me."

When Emma had taken all she needed from this past life and found inner peace, she went back outside and found Hector waiting to take her back. Shanty was also there and smiled. I asked if Shanty could help release any shadow or residual trauma from this lifetime, allowing Emma to have that peace now.

Emma took in a very deep breath and let it out slowly. "I feel like a weight has been lifted off my head and shoulders." She touched the very center of her forehead. "The shadows of the forest have moved. Now there is light."

I guided Emma gently back out of trance. When she was fully back, she took a moment and then said, "It feels so peaceful now, like something physical had been removed from my body. I feel free—mentally and physically. I understand I need to put myself first more. What was that, though? I heard myself speaking in another language!?"

Later that day, Emma sent me a text saying she had fallen asleep after our session. She added, "I kept getting this name in my head; it wouldn't go away. I looked it up… it was the name of my tribe—

Umpqua—and they actually really existed. I am gobsmacked. Absolutely gobsmacked right now."

I love when sessions like this reveal how much deeper our subconscious memory runs than we often realize. Emma's experience reminds me of how healing doesn't just happen in the mind—it happens across lifetimes, across lineages, across the very fabric of who we are.

What stood out to me most here was the presence of guides—Hector, the impish forest companion, and Shanty, the healer. Often, when clients meet figures like these, they wonder if they are "real." Are they archetypes, symbolic protectors, or actual spiritual presences? My perspective is that it doesn't matter which explanation you lean toward. What matters is that the subconscious chooses these exact images and beings to walk us through what we need to see, feel, and release. The symbolism alone can be profoundly transformative.

The feather in this story is such a striking example. Given to Emma in trance, and later recognized as a thread between her healing experience and her remembered past life, it became a bridge between subconscious and conscious awareness. Objects like this often show up in sessions—a scroll, a key, a stone, a feather—and they anchor the healing in something tangible that the conscious mind can hold onto afterward. It's as though the subconscious leaves breadcrumbs, so we don't lose the thread once we return to waking awareness.

And then there's the chanting. Many clients are startled when unfamiliar languages or sounds pour through them during hypnosis. But these experiences are ancient, often encoded in the body's memory. They don't need translation to be effective. The language of vibration, rhythm, and sound reaches beyond words into the cellular and energetic levels where true healing occurs.

What I find most moving about Emma's journey is how it closed with recognition. The name "Umpqua" surfacing in her mind, refusing to let go until she looked it up, gave her conscious confirmation that what she had touched wasn't "just imagination." It was an ancestral memory. It was the body remembering. It was her soul saying, this is real, this is yours, and this is where healing continues.

Sessions like this remind me why QJH isn't only about hypnosis techniques or scripts. It's about being willing to witness and honor whatever arises—be it angels, ancestors, archetypes, or unfamiliar languages—and trust that the subconscious is guiding us to exactly what needs to be reclaimed.

~Kryssa

Part Two: The Tribe Remembered

By Nikki Hoare

Emma (not her real name) had a previous QJH session with me, and this time was interested in visiting her Temple of Healing to see if she could meet her inner healer and gain some physical healing and inner peace.

When in trance, Emma did not go to her healing temple. Instead, after surrounding herself in a protective bubble, she found herself walking along a path in a forest. There was a presence—a small, impish chap standing on the path. He was called Hector, dressed in animal furs with a leaf hat. He was about the size of a child and carried a cane made from a branch.

Hector led Emma through the forest to a house, triangular in shape, covered in moss and ivy. The door was made from a tree trunk. (Emma physically held up her hand to touch it.) As she did, she told me that she was expected and that she should go inside.

Inside the house, she described what she could see: "Lots of candles, beautiful light everywhere, warm.

There is an old-fashioned bed covered in animal furs."

There was an old Aboriginal woman with grey hair, wearing animal furs. She was beautiful. Emma asked who she was. Her name was "Shanty," a healer.

Shanty guided Emma to lie down on the bed and began to move her hands over Emma, gently touching her chest, face, and head. (Emma indicated the places as she spoke by touching them with her own hands.)

Other women came into the room and stood around the bed. Emma said she felt like she was floating, a warm sensation like an energy pulsing through her body. Then Emma began to chant in another language. Her voice was quieter, softer, reaching her hands out wide as she chanted.

Then Emma said that Shanty and the other women were cleansing her—wrapping her with soil and herbs, sage and rosemary. "I know those smells," Emma said, wiping her own hands across her body as she spoke. She then started to tap out a beat on her leg, chanting again in the same foreign language as before.

After a short while, Emma became quiet and still. Then she said there was a knock at the door. Shanty opened it to find Hector standing there. Shanty turned and gave Emma a large feather before Emma left with Hector.

Emma said she understood now—she had been here before, a very long time ago. Another lifetime. This was her home. She was a Native American Indian—she could see it now. She had long dark hair, and she was dancing around a fire. "It's my wedding day, and I have a feather in my hair. It looks like the same feather I was given before."

There was a sense of community; children were playing and laughing. She continued to describe the village and the surroundings. They were by a river. The buildings were solid but could be packed up and moved.

Emma began to cry. "I am in my early twenties. There is a familiar feel to one particular tepee. Inside, there is a fire and pots. I reach out my hands as if to hug someone—Mama."

"I am home. My name is Gannowa. Mama is telling me to be at peace, that I can come back for healing anytime. Oh—I died in childbirth. That was a burial ritual—my burial. Mama shows me that my bones are with them. I will go with them always. I see my child.

She is beautiful, and they have called her Gannowa after me."

When Emma had taken all she needed from this past life and found inner peace, she went back outside and found Hector waiting to take her back. Shanty was also there and smiled. I asked if Shanty could help release any shadow or residual trauma from this lifetime, allowing Emma to have that peace now.

Emma took in a very deep breath and let it out slowly. "I feel like a weight has been lifted off my head and shoulders." She touched the very center of her forehead. "The shadows of the forest have moved. Now there is light."

I guided Emma gently back out of trance. When she was fully back, she took a moment and then said, "It feels so peaceful now, like something physical had been removed from my body. I feel free—mentally and physically. I understand I need to put myself first more. What was that, though? I heard myself speaking in another language!?"

Later that day, Emma sent me a text saying she had fallen asleep after our session. She added, "I kept getting this name in my head; it wouldn't go away. I looked it up… it was the name of my tribe—

Umpqua—and they actually really existed. I am gobsmacked. Absolutely gobsmacked right now."

There's something awe-inspiring about a session that reveals details that later prove to have a basis in recorded history. Stories like Emma's remind us that the line between imagination, memory, and ancestral connection is not as fixed as we've been taught. Whether you believe she accessed a literal past life, ancestral memory stored in the body, or the collective unconscious, what matters is the healing that followed.

Her chanting in a language she didn't consciously know, the sensation of herbs and soil, the deep grief of childbirth, and the discovery of the Umpqua tribe afterwards— these moments are powerful reminders that we carry echoes within us. Sometimes they show up as fears or pains that don't make sense in this lifetime. Other times, they emerge as a strange familiarity with a culture, a landscape, or even a word we shouldn't know but somehow do.

What touches me most in this story is Emma's realization that the shadows lifted, and light returned. Healing at this depth isn't just symbolic—it's felt in the body, in the release of weight and pressure we may not have realized we were carrying. Whether you call that soul memory, epigenetics, or spirit, the effect is the same: we walk away lighter, freer, and more at peace.

~Kryssa

From the client's perspective

A Student Discovers Quantum Journeys Hypnosis and Enjoys a First Session

By Anonymous

Discovering QJH has been quite the journey for me personally. Although it is not advertised or promoted as 'spiritual', I was already on my spiritual path and wanted to progress this, so for me, it has been very spiritual, which is exactly what I wanted and needed.

I believe I was drawn to it for a reason. After many, many years of wanting to go back into doing hypnosis -after losing my confidence- I came across the course and found that it resonated with me more than any of the multiple hypnosis/hypnotherapy courses I had previously done. Having my own sessions from one of the QJH students blew my mind, and I was able to work through blockages, gain wisdom and insight, and develop a strong connection to my Higher-Self.

My higher-self gave me advice to meditate with crystals to connect more with her, which I did, and I am now able to connect whenever I am in need of guidance and support. I have also been drawn to other fascinating avenues to explore that I never knew existed, such as spirit release therapy, and have begun to work on and see progress in developing my skills in mediumship and psychic abilities.

This was my first session, the start of amazing things!

I went floating through space and met my Higher-Self, a beautiful angel called Seraphina. In the session, my aim was to work through the blockages to feel confident and to start practicing hypnotherapy again after many years of having somehow lost that confidence.

We asked my Higher-Self what I needed to know or do to overcome it. She said I can't heal others because I'm not healed myself. She said all the mess inside me needs cleaning up, all the broken bits inside me need healing, and the light needs to be put back in. I imagined lots of broken, sharp glass inside me, and she filed down all the jagged edges. She swept all the sharp edges out with a brush and then cleansed it with healing water, making it smooth and healed so that it couldn't hurt anybody. She then filled me up with healing golden light.

I realised then that the light had gone from me a long time ago, when I was a child, and everything had broken. I recognised the light when she put it back in. I felt all happy and giggly like a child. She filled me up with the light until it was shining out of me like I was a star or a glitter ball. She also held my hands so I could feel the love I hadn't felt when I was little. She told me I could put the light back in myself anytime I want to; I don't need to wait for her to do it.

I can just look at the moon or sun as they are always there, and the light is in them, so if there are ever any blocks, I can just look at the moon or sun and put the light back in myself. She also said to keep better connection and communication with her. I needed to meditate for 10 minutes a day with crystals.

She said she had always been there, but we had lost touch for such a long time. She agreed to increase the % of connection I have with her. She did this by 10 percent. She didn't want to increase it too quickly as she knows I'm fiercely independent and like to do things by myself, so she wanted me to feel I was doing things for myself and take the credit for it myself, which she said is important for my confidence to grow. She said she will always be there, but she won't interfere- I can ask for help when I need it.

At the start of the session, the hallway was huge, and I couldn't see to the end of it... when we went back into the hall at the end, it looked lighter, as if the lights had come on, and it didn't look so big and overwhelming, which is exactly how I felt about the prospect of starting hypnotherapy again.

I truly feel like hypnosis is my calling and that QJH called me specifically.

Every QJHA student who enrolls also gives and receives 6 sessions as part of the mandatory requirements to graduate, but many continue to give and receive sessions on an as-needed basis with their favorite QJH colleagues.

We do this for the obvious reason of knowing that the more we practice, the more comfortable we'll be with the protocol in our sessions with clients. But we also do this so that we heal the aspects of ourselves that might be afraid of failure, or conversely, afraid of success.

We address self-sabotage, imposter syndrome, and that funny thing that so many of us have where we never feel quite good enough or knowledgeable enough, so we purchase course after course after course in the hopes that one day we'll magically feel like we're ENOUGH.

There's a saying that goes, "You can't give from an empty cup". And so, QJHA students receive many opportunities to work on, release, or resolve their own issues in order to better help our clients.

~Kryssa

Quantum Healing Journey Reflection

By Tiani Perkins

I came to Kryssa in July 2022 for a Quantum Journeys Healing session because I was struggling to understand what the next steps I should take in life were. I was feeling very torn between a few different directions that my life was pulling me in. But I couldn't trust myself enough or my instincts enough to know which life path I needed to follow. I was at a job that I felt was really not a good fit for me anymore, and it was causing me loads of anxiety, exhaustion, and confusion.

During my Quantum Journey, I felt extremely relaxed and safe. I didn't feel sleepy, but rather, almost in an autopilot state, where my mind didn't need to think in order to function properly. My body felt light, and outside distractions just didn't faze me.

Kryssa took me to meet with my Inner Healer. Her name was Ahmana, and she was a sweet, elderly Native American woman. I didn't speak her language, but for some reason, I seemed to simply understand her innately. This guide of mine took me to a large spread of foods and supplements that would support my health and my thyroid condition, and she showed me which foods to avoid for optimal health.

After connecting with my Inner Healer, I went ahead to the Hallway of Answers, where I met my Highest-Self, Joseph. Actually, I didn't meet him…I became him. I was somehow channeling his infinite wisdom, and Kryssa began to ask him the questions that I had presented to her before starting our session. My voice became low and deep, like a man's. And the intonations I was using lacked excitement. I was speaking in a very dry and matter-of-fact tone, which is the exact opposite of my normally very animated and excited expressions.

While channeling my Highest-Self, Joseph answered the questions presented to him by Kryssa on my behalf. When asked what my life would look like in one year, he shared that it would be too different for my mind to comprehend. So even though he couldn't share the details of my future with me, he provided Kryssa with very specific directions for me to follow in order to uncover the next steps I should take. I was to meditate every day for 40 days straight on the word 'Trust'. This meditation session was to be 30 minutes long and would begin at 8:20 am every morning.

I had also shared with Kryssa that my husband and I had been clashing a ton around that time, so she asked Joseph if he could speak to my husband's Highest-Self so that we might better understand what would serve us as a couple. However, to my surprise, his Highest-Self declined to speak with us because she was too busy protecting him at the moment and keeping him in a safe container. Joseph was able to glance over, and I could see my husband inside a large force field of energy, balled up in the fetal position, isolating himself from the rest of the world. I wasn't at all surprised to see that image because the way he was presented in our day-to-day lives was similar.

So, we concluded the session shortly after, and I returned to my full awareness with a memory of the entire session. I felt refreshed and so much lighter than when we had begun the session. Kryssa informed me that I may not remember much from the session, but that my mind and body would retain all the necessary information.

The next day, I headed to the local health food market and purchased all the food items that Ahmana advised me to eat. And I began the meditation ritual that Joseph prescribed to me. And over the next few months after my QH session, my life began to shift just ever so slightly.

Communication and connection with my husband were back to our loving and supportive normal interactions. When the contract for my job ended, I stood tall in my decision not to renew. I've since discovered an elimination diet that has nearly reversed my hypothyroidism and adrenal glands. And now, nearly nine months after my session with Kryssa, I have so much more energy than I've had in years. I haven't felt this clear-minded, healthy, and strong in a long time. I truly didn't know it would ever be possible for me to feel this youthful again.

I have so much more energy to play with my kids. I'm exercising again after years of too much exhaustion to work out. I've tapped into my manifestation powers again – which I thought had disappeared for good now that I was an adult. I've relaunched my hypnotherapy business, and I've just hit my very first $5,000 month, which was unfathomable to me just a few months ago.

All of these changes have been so easy and organic. I didn't have to force myself to make the changes after my session; it was as though my body was still on autopilot after my session with Kryssa. It's as if I've been slowly, magnetically drawn to the life that I'm meant to be living.

My Quantum Healing Journey changed the entire trajectory of my life in more facets than I could have ever imagined. This protocol is such a gentle yet extraordinarily powerful tool for inner healing and transformation.

What I love about this session is how beautifully it shows the ripple effect of trusting inner wisdom. Sometimes the answers aren't given in a way our logical minds want—step-by-step instructions with guarantees—but rather as practices that build the muscle of trust itself. The guidance to meditate daily on one word, "Trust," was deceptively simple, yet it became the key that unlocked everything else. Healing her body, strengthening her marriage, releasing a job that was no longer aligned— all of it began to fall into place naturally, without forcing. That's the magic of this work: when we align, life reorganizes around that alignment.

And sometimes the journey doesn't stop at personal healing. For this client, the changes were so profound and life-giving that she chose to carry this work forward, becoming a professional *Quantum Journeys Hypnotist* herself. It's one of the greatest joys for me as a teacher to watch someone move from uncertainty and struggle into clarity and empowerment—and then take those tools to help others find their way home too.

~Kryssa

Procrastination For Healing

By Henriette Kern-Schuh

Once, I had an interesting QJH session with a dear colleague whom I had consulted because of some chronic physical issues, for which there seemed to be no remedy.

She asked me what I would like most to release. My answer was, of course: My symptoms.

To the question of what I would like most to acquire, I told her: Health, physical strength, and more fun in life. I also told her that I would like to understand why my body didn't want to function anymore like it did and what I could do in order to improve my situation. She asked me to describe what my life would be like when I had reached my goals.

Then we started the Quantum Journey. After leaving my conscious mind in my Happy Safe Place on a lovely beach, my hypnotist, Katie, led me to the Hallway of Answers. This time, it looked like a kind of cave or a dwarf's home dug into the earth. She suggested looking directly for the Temple of Healing in order to get advice from my Inner Healer and take advantage of some special healing treatments.

The Temple of Healing was a large, dark cave, and my Inner Healer had the appearance of Buddha sitting on a kind of throne. After listening carefully to me explaining my perception of the illness and the symptoms, my Inner Healer recommended that I slow down my pace and my expectations of myself. Otherwise, my body would continue to force me to do so.

He also talked about helpful exercises that I could do in order to get some relief. I told him that I couldn't motivate myself to perform them, I never found the right time and place, and had a lot of other things with more priority to do during the day. So, he suggested having a conversation with my Inner Procrastinating Part.

Unfortunately, this part was quite reluctant. It looked like a little red devil called Max. And it didn't want to change its mind, as it felt responsible for providing me with sufficient rest, which it thought was to my highest good. At first, we asked for help, and an army of soldiers appeared, prepared to arrest the little devil and thus prevent it from disturbing me any longer. But then my Higher-Self made the objection that this wasn't a good idea because it would get very angry and possibly come back with worse symptoms.

While we were wondering what to do with Max, suddenly my Inner Pride Part arrived in the shape of a slim and sporty young lady, who explained the importance of staying attractive and in good shape as I get older. This part convinced the little devil that people who rest too much are not able to stay flexible, physically fit, and healthy. Finally, the Procrastinating Part agreed to allow for sufficient rest during the night only and allowed some exercise at special times of the day. They both went away hand in hand, and my Inner Healer Buddha was satisfied as well. However, he recommended that I take a Shower of Healing Light, which was supposed to help me with my actual issues and pain. This was wonderful, I felt really repaired, healed, and rejuvenated afterward.

After this impressive experience, Katie led me back to my Happy Safe Place and then emerged me from hypnosis, while giving me strengthening suggestions to increase its effectiveness. QJH is full of efficient content that the subconscious mind can choose from for any physical or psychological issues or problems.

I absolutely love when a client's inner parts show up in such vivid, symbolic ways. Here, procrastination wasn't just an abstract idea— it had a name, a face, and even a stubborn personality. That's the beauty of parts work

256

inside QJH: we get to interact with aspects of ourselves in a way that feels concrete, playful, and surprisingly honest.

And what's even better is that solutions don't always come through force—sometimes another part, like Pride in this case, can step in to negotiate balance. It's such a perfect reminder that even our so-called "negative" parts are usually trying to protect us in the only way they know how.

What stands out most to me is how this session reflects the adaptability of the subconscious. Rather than eliminating procrastination (which could have led to backlash), the inner wisdom of this client allowed for compromise—rest at night, activity during the day.

That balance, paired with the Shower of Healing Light, created a shift that felt not only healing but sustainable. These are the kinds of sessions that show us we don't have to fight against ourselves; we can learn to listen, collaborate, and realign so that all parts of us can finally work together.

~Kryssa

Finding My Life Purpose with QJH

By Henriette Kern-Schuh

During my QJH live training, I had a session as a client with a highly esteemed colleague. I had several subjects on my list for which I wished to get insights, e.g.

"What is my mission in this life?"

"Why did I choose my parents?"

"Why do I feel an obligation to help everybody?"

"What am I supposed to specialize in as a life coach?"

I decided to ask for answers to my first question.

Our intention was to enter the Hallway of Answers and then go through the door to the Akasha Records, which you can imagine as a huge library where everything is recorded about anything happening in the world. After the induction to deep hypnosis, I sent my conscious mind to sleep in my Happy Safe Place, a nice little place at the beach, surrounded by palm trees, lying on a sunbed on a lazy afternoon. The sun went down slowly but still gave enough warmth to feel cozy and in total relaxation.

Meanwhile, my hypnotist led my subconscious mind to the hallway of answers. Every time the hallway looked different, I was curious about how it would be this time. It turned out to be a big hallway like in a castle, splendid and magnificent, held in white, decorated with lots of gold. The many doors on both sides were red. All of them were closed except one at the end of the hall on the right side. I was drawn to it, inviting me to enter. I wondered what was awaiting me behind it.

I had been told that it could be difficult to enter the Akasha Records directly, and you sometimes had to overcome obstacles to find it. But I was lucky and found myself in a spacious library with an incredible number of books. I couldn't even see the end of the shelves. So how could I know which book contained the answer I was hoping for?

Suddenly, my Higher-Self appeared as a fairy, completely dressed in white. She looked at me in a very friendly manner and showed me a big book with a wooden cover in dark green, with my name written on it in golden letters. I opened the book to any page. To my astonishment, it was more like a photo album with pictures of my childhood. The pictures showed either my parents or me, but never all of us together. My mother's face never seemed to show happiness.

Also, my smile looked somewhat forced, as if it were only for the photo.

For your information, I was separated from my parents for 2.5 years (from ages 4 to 6 and a half years old). They left the country, leaving me behind. After we had been reunited, I was no longer able to have a loving relationship with them. And they made a lot of unreasonable decisions, which ruined them financially and burdened their marriage.

I remember that as a child, I often could foresee the outcome of their actions. But I never told them, anyway, they wouldn't have listened to me. When I grew older, my mother often involved me in their conflicts, asking me to mediate between her and my father. The moment I realised how unpleasant this had been for me, I said all at once, "Enough of the old things," and closed the book.

The insight I got from all these memories gave me the answer to all of my questions. My mission in life is to help people cope with their stress and problems. I chose my parents in order to learn the necessary skills for that. Especially to help my clients have fulfilling relationships or to leave toxic ones, whichever they most need. I suddenly became aware that, for whatever issues my clients came to see me, at a certain time, we landed on the subject of their relationship, or lovesickness, or loneliness. I had often dealt with this myself, almost incidentally.

Up to that point, I had always worked with only one partner. This is definitely very helpful because when one person changes his or her attitude and behavior, the other persons in the family or in the conflict will change automatically as well. But now I suddenly could see myself in a coaching situation with both, doing marriage counseling and mediation. It was a future pace, a kind of Quantum Jump.

So, finally, I got all of my questions answered just because they were on my list. That was a lot more than I had expected. It was the most enlightening and amazing hypnosis session I've ever had. By the way, the day after that, I booked a mediation class to learn how to work with two conflicting parties.

Sessions like this highlight one of the most profound gifts of hypnosis: the ability to step outside of old stories long enough to see them clearly. In everyday life, we often rehash memories through the same filter we've always carried—shame, guilt, or resignation. But in trance, we can revisit the same memories from a higher vantage point, with the support of our Higher-self. That's when everything shifts. Here, the Akasha Records provided not just symbolic imagery, but a mirror: childhood photos that revealed patterns of absence, tension, and forced smiles. When she declared, "Enough of the old things," she wasn't just closing a book—she was closing the loop on a cycle of inherited stress and misplaced responsibility.

What's so powerful is how these insights ripple into purpose. Hypnosis doesn't just help us heal; it helps us understand why we are the way we are *and how that wiring can actually be part of our mission. This client realized that her early experiences uniquely prepared her to help others navigate conflict and relationships. That's the beauty of this work: pain is transformed into wisdom, and wisdom becomes service. The subconscious doesn't just release—it redirects, opening up entirely new paths forward, sometimes so clearly that the very next day you find yourself signing up for a meditation class that feels like destiny.*

~Kryssa

My Journey to Becoming a QJH Practitioner

By Lorraine Dodder

Right before I qualified as a QJH Practitioner, I experienced a wonderful session. I had no expectations and truly just surrendered to the moment.

During the session, we are taken to a happy, safe place and then into our Hallway of Answers. As soon as I entered, I found myself in a Greek/Roman-type bath. There were columns entwined with vines. It was a beautiful, serene place, and I felt completely at peace and safe. I found myself in the pool with several other goddess-like and beautiful women who were bathing me and washing my hair. It felt like a very poignant and sacred moment. The water was filled with rose petals, and it smelled divine. It felt as if I was getting ready for something very special indeed.

Next, the women helped me out of the pool and proceeded to rub rose oil all over me and dressed me in a white toga, then they coffered my hair and led me to a very large doorway, over 20 feet tall, I would say. The doors opened, and four men, two on either side, lined the doors. Feels weird to say, but I seemed important, and they bowed their heads in reverence as I walked by.

Next, I was led into a chamber, and my deceased Mum, Nan, and my late partner were standing in front of me. They were laughing and smiling! It was wonderful to see them. I became very emotional; they all comforted me, and we had a few private words.

Then, out of nowhere, a wizard-like man appeared who told me his name was Merlin. He ushered me towards a large table, and upon it was an array of ornate wands, some small, some large, all different colours. Merlin asked me to choose one, and I chose a long gold one. Merlin imparted knowledge and guidance to me and led me to a smaller chamber. In the corner, there was an eagle watching, and it felt like they were overseeing this sacred moment. An eagle represents a sacred messenger between humans and the spirit realm, so this was a lovely message to receive.

Merlin then proceeded to ask me to lay on a stone plinth to receive healing and a kind of energy upgrade. He produced a green laser, which kind of reminded me of a cheese cutter, which seemed quite amusing at the time. I received healing, and he bid me goodbye.

What I took from the session was that this was a kind of initiation and energy upgrade. Afterward, I had many clients who were able to gain entry into the Akashic Records, other dimensions, and much more.

Since qualifying as a Quantum Journeys Practitioner, I have had many clients who have achieved incredible healing journeys where they have tried a myriad of other therapies, none of which have worked. QJH has helped them completely heal from long-term OCD (30 years), autoimmune issues, severe anxiety, chronic overthinking, and much more. Most results have been achieved in just one session, powerful stuff, right?

This session reads like an initiation, and in many ways, that's exactly what it was. The subconscious often uses rich archetypal imagery to mark thresholds in our personal evolution. Here, the Greek/Roman bath wasn't just a backdrop—it symbolized purification and preparation. The goddess-like women, the rose oil, the ceremonial dressing—all pointed to a rite of passage. What's fascinating is that Lorraine's subconscious gave her an initiation experience at precisely the moment she was preparing to step into her new role as a practitioner. It's a beautiful example of how the inner world mirrors the outer.

Merlin's appearance is also worth noting. In hypnosis, guides often show up in ways that resonate with our personal mythologies. For some, it might be Jesus, for others, a grandmother, and for Lorraine, it was Merlin—an archetype of wisdom, transformation, and magical authority.

His offering of the wand was a symbolic passing of power, affirming her readiness to step into her own role as healer. The "energy upgrade" she received echoes what many clients describe as a recalibration, almost like the nervous system is being rewired to hold more light, more awareness, and more capacity.

What I love most is how these symbolic experiences translate into real-world impact. After this session, Lorraine noticed a marked shift in her clients' journeys, with deeper access to the Akashic Records and profound healing outcomes.

This is what makes QJH so extraordinary: the inner initiations aren't just metaphorical—they ripple out into our practice, our relationships, and our results with clients. When the subconscious gives us a ceremony like this, it isn't just a dream. It's a blueprint for the healer we are becoming.

~Kryssa

How QJH Helped Me to Overcome the Hardest Period of My Life

By Joelle Anthony

In December 2023, I booked an appointment with a QJH therapist. I had in the past seen a "regular" hypnotist, and after five sessions, this had come to nothing. I never once felt hypnotised, and although I felt that talking to the hypnotist must have done some good, it didn't work in the long term.

I had been struggling emotionally in the last four and a half years after moving to France to help take care of my mother, who was crumbling away to Parkinson's, untreatable. My siblings put her in a "care" home just before COVID appeared, and OAPs were abandoned. I was living in a 45m2 flat with no garden and one bedroom to share with my teenage daughter. She had developed a massive ovarian tumour cancer and was put through three rounds of chemotherapy, ending in an important operation.

Six months later, my mum passed. Quite a chunk to handle emotionally, and being single, I had no one to really rely on or to turn to in tough times.

With all the spiritual learning that I had researched since the 2010s, I had only recently heard of QJH but didn't really know what exactly it meant. I booked an appointment, hoping that it might bring some "unblocking" to my day-to-day life. It was one of the best decisions I have ever made!

Between the undeniable feeling of "butterflies in my tummy" as I reached the Hallway of Answers, the Higher-Self that felt so caring and loving, the "past life" that I was observing, and then the knowledge of me being in a triangular spaceship high above, with a uniform and a metallic table surrounded by very bright light, just waiting…. Nothing felt odd. It was just a very calm observation. I can't recall everything, and the footage of the session was never recorded. But the immediate outcome was a great feeling of relief that we are not alone, that we are all loved, that we are all part of the greater oneness. That whatever happens is also for a reason, and that we can make our future much better if we just trust, believe, and want to care.

A month after the appointment, I had a call from a town nearby saying that they had a four-bed house with a garden appointed for us! It is spacious and luminous, just as I had wished for! My relationships with family and friends have changed, and I feel more like I am around others. My feelings of loneliness have gone, and my spiritual beliefs have massively grown. I signed up for Kryssa Marie Bowman's Transformative Hypnotherapy Training course. I even subscribed to the week of intensive Training!

I have always felt a calling to the more spiritual world, and that awakening after the session with Lorraine Dodder was the best proof that it is time to change and create!

Stories like Joelle's show the difference between "trying to be hypnotized" and actually experiencing a Quantum Journeys session. Traditional hypnosis can be incredibly effective, but QJH goes beyond suggestion—it opens a doorway into connection with the Higher-self. That's why Joelle could feel the butterflies in her tummy, sense the loving presence of her Higher-self, and step into scenes that held both symbolic and cosmic meaning.

None of it felt odd to her because it was flowing directly from her own subconscious, not something imposed from the outside. This is the real power of the work: it creates a safe and expansive space for whatever healing or perspective the soul is ready to access.

What I especially love is how the transformation rippled into Joelle's everyday life. Within a month, she had moved into the kind of home she'd been longing for, felt her loneliness dissolve, and experienced a renewal of both her relationships and her spiritual calling. These are the kinds of shifts that often feel miraculous, but they come from within— when the blocks lift, life itself begins to reorganize around that new freedom. And just like so many others who have felt this deep change, Joelle has chosen to carry it forward by stepping into training herself. That's how the circle continues: from healing, to awakening, to becoming the one who holds space for others.

~Kryssa

Meeting Draco

By Nikki Hoare

My first experience of Quantum Journeys Hypnosis as a participant was when I took part in a group session to visit The Healing Temple run by Kryssa. I was not sure what to expect at first, despite my training in QJH, as I do not usually manage to visualise when in hypnosis, but as I settled down and started to listen to Kryssa guiding us, I was pleasantly surprised to notice I had flashes of images. What I experienced is still fresh to me now. I considered what I wanted to get from the experience.

I wanted to release any tension and learn how to take care of myself and my well-being. I am also looking to relieve the discomfort in my legs from my varicose veins. I had to have a vein stripped out several years ago when one of the valves ruptured. Since then, I have experienced stiffness and tenderness in them and a soreness like a bruise. Which comes and goes over the month; some days are better than others.

As I approached my Happy Safe place, I found myself feeling a great sense of calm. At first, my senses picked up a range of colours, from different shades of blue and green to yellow. These swirled around and started to settle, and I realised that I was looking out across the ocean on a sunny day. The beach was a soft, golden sand, and I could imagine hearing the soft, gentle sounds of the waves. Then, I became aware of a wooden cabin to one side with a porchway and trees surrounding it. There was a hammock between the trees to which I found myself drawn.

Moving on up to the Hallway of Answers to visit the Temple of Healing was like traveling through some sort of portal with traveling lines that seemed to spiral and flow with me, guiding me onwards. When I entered through the doorway leading to my healing temple, I found myself at the bottom of a mountain with lush green plants hanging around the entrance. In the distance, I could hear the faint sound of a waterfall. As I became more aware of things around me, I also became aware of a presence behind me.

Under the guidance of Kryssa, I asked this presence to come forward so I could see it more clearly and introduce it. I started to notice scales, a large body, and the shuffling sounds of something moving. Then its eyes seemed to appear bright blue with a deep feeling of compassion and safety.

As this presence moved around me, I realised it was a dragon and he was called Draco. He spoke to me and said that he was going to take me up to the temple.

The next thing I registered or felt was the wind blowing past me and the feeling of flying, holding on, but still knowing I was safe. This was an incredible feeling. I started to look around and noticed we were flying up the side of the mountain, past the trees. Noticing, far below, various waterfalls cascading down into one another. Houses and monuments are scattered among the trees. At the top was a temple with beautiful white marble columns and steps. Food was laid out across a large table to one side, with lots of wonderful fresh fruits and vegetables and many interesting dishes. As my mind took in all the different foods, some started to fade away, some floated off the end of the table, out of sight, and others shrank down small.

Somehow, I just knew and understood that this was showing me what foods were good for me and which to reduce or remove from my diet. Moving on, I came to an area of extreme calmness and became aware of a different sensation flowing over my body. As it did, I became more and more relaxed; it felt like a weight was lifted, and warmth filled the space.

After a while, I felt it was time to move on and felt guided over to the side where there was a waterfall. As I watched the shimmering waters cascade into the pool, I became aware of some steps leading into the water. I then became aware of the sensation of the waters flowing over me, cooling, yet just the right temperature. Easing and soothing every part of me, reaching into the very heart of me, every muscle, every nerve. I could sense that any stress, tension, or discomfort held within my body was being washed away. Looking down at my feet, I could see different shades of deep blue and purple washing away and washing out of me. I stayed there until the waters ran completely clear again and felt an incredible sense of ease and comfort, of lightness.

After a while, I found myself flying back down the mountain to the doorway, back into the hallway. Just before leaving my inner healer, Draco spoke again, telling me that I could always come back any time. I just needed to think of my beach and call out his name, and he will be there. When I came out of the experience, I had such a sense of calmness and happiness, along with my wonder at where all that had just come from. It was like nothing I had ever experienced before.

From time to time, when I want to take a bit of time for myself or reconnect my mind and body in that healing way, I take myself to the beach and reach out to Draco. Over time, I have indeed noticed that my legs have been a lot better and more comfortable. I am able to enjoy going for walks with the family again and not have a throbbing ache because of it. My legs are not tired and heavy at the end of the day. This has definitely been an experience I will not forget.

One of the things I always love about guiding group journeys is that people often go in thinking, "I'm not sure I can visualize"—and then they surprise themselves with vivid experiences that feel more real than imagined.

That's because hypnosis isn't about "trying" to see something; it's about allowing the subconscious to communicate in the way it knows best. For some, that's images. For others, it's sensations, sounds, or simply a deep knowing. What stands out in this story is the appearance of Draco, the dragon guide. For many, an inner healer or guide shows up in human form, but sometimes it's an animal, a symbol, or—like here—a mythical being. The subconscious has an extraordinary way of presenting what feels most protective, safe, and powerful for that person. And what a gift Draco gave: not only guidance in the temple, but also the promise of returning anytime simply by calling his name.

I also love how the imagery wove practical healing together with symbolic release. The foods on the table shifting and disappearing gave clear direction about nourishment, while the waterfall washing away blue and purple shades of pain gave the body a direct experience of release. This is why people often notice physical improvements after sessions—they've rehearsed healing so fully in the subconscious that the body begins following suit.

The beauty of QJH is that these experiences are not just "once in a lifetime." Like this participant discovered, you can return again and again—on a walk, in meditation, or even in the middle of a stressful day—simply by revisiting your Happy Safe Place and reconnecting with the guide who showed up for you.

~Kryssa

Relearning to Love Myself

By Terri Schmidt

By the time I experienced my own Quantum Journey, I had taken most of the QJH classes. I was already a certified hypnotist and wanted to expand my scope of knowledge into the quantum realm. I found that because the QJH process is so flexible and client-led, I could enter into the session without hesitation.

The intake portion of the session revealed that I wanted to release the sense of lack in terms of finances and in terms of not being or having enough. I wanted to acquire a whole sense of how I would serve my clients. I wanted to understand how I could move forward and accomplish something with a sense of ease and purpose. I wanted to transform the feeling of guessing so I could have more assurance with decisions.

Miracle Question: How will I know? I will have clients. I'll serve people more regularly, and messaging will be easier. What would I most like to ask my Higher-Self and/or guides? How do I maintain integrity and monetize this as I am serving people? My happy, safe place is not one I have ever imagined before, nor is it a place I can remember being. I am in the woods by a brook that has clear, clean water and smooth stones. The tall trees provide filtered light and gentle shade. It's so peaceful listening to the sounds of the water and songbirds. It is morning here, and the air is crisp, yet comfortable. A cozy blanket is waiting for me under a huge shade tree, where I wrap myself up like a cocoon and allow it to rock me back and forth, deeper and deeper. I feel so safe, so protected. This is where I am instructed by the facilitator to leave my waking consciousness to rest while my Higher-Self continues the journey, leaving all the doubts, questions, and worries behind.

I seem to float above the scene, tethered by a long, silver cord. I drift higher up from the earth plane to an expansive place. I find myself in a hallway that has no doors on either side. There is a beautiful, blueish light at the end of this hallway, and it begins pulling me as if I were on a fast-moving walkway. I am not doing the walking. I am being moved ahead very quickly toward the light. The facilitator suggests I check to see that I am still connected to that silver cord; I am. She asks if I feel safe to proceed; I do. I feel perfectly safe. And now the light in the hallway is dimmer. I am no longer being pulled forward. The blue light becomes lighter, and it shows the threshold of a doorway. The facilitator asked me if I wanted to have a guide or healer take me through it, but I wanted to go through it on my own. She said to ask the blue light if it was safe for me to enter. As I do, the blue light becomes white, and I feel a sensation of being pulled forward through the doorway. There are misty shadows moving within the light. But it is comfortable. I'm in a roundish room. There are two giant hands standing vertically, touching each other at the fingertips and the wrists. I am to walk through them.

Facilitator: "It's a room? Where are you?"

Me: "A space. It is Consciousness, unfamiliar, wisdom."

Facilitator: "Pure consciousness?"

Me: "I don't know."

Facilitator: "Is there anyone there who wants to come forward and speak with you?"

Me: "Arms. Love. There is someone."

Although I do not see who might be there giving me this great sense of love, my attention is turned to something that resembles a totem pole carved of wood. One image with facial features going up the pole and one going down in the opposite direction is like a reflection, but not a reflection. There is a light in the center that separates the two images. I don't know what to make of it, but it has a strong presence. Suddenly, I'm in a tunnel. And I'm moving in the tunnel as if I were on a ride at an amusement park, and there's water beneath me in that tunnel, like a stream that is reflecting light. I'm moving so fast. I turn to the right and to the left, but I am not really able to see much. Golden-orange lighting highlights the shape of the tunnel. It feels as if I'm underground or in a cave of some kind. The totem pole had vanished, perhaps before I began the journey through the tunnel.

I stop. There is a big, arched wooden door with a large metal handle.

The facilitator says that on the other side of the door, there will be something very significant for everything I want to learn, understand, and transform today. Giving gratitude, I open the door and walk over the threshold. I see a smooth ceiling and light colors. I do not see walls, but I know they are there. I see a desk with a leather top and a pen, a drawer with three divided sections, and a key inside one of the sections. Taking the key, I look around the room. I see a chest. It is my grandmother's cedar chest, the one at the foot of my bed. I use the key to open it.

Facilitator: "What's in there (the chest)?"

"Answers. The answers are in there for me. They are all for me. And as silly as it sounds, they are all like animated letters spelling the word 'ANSWERS'. So many of them!"

The facilitator then says, "So let's ask this ethereal chest for answers on how we might release any sense of lack, of unworthiness, or lack of abundance. How can this be released into the consciousness? Starting now."

At once, the top of my head opens up, and the words begin flowing from the chest into my head, one by one. They just keep coming, one 'ANSWER' after another. To me, it seems like it's lasting several minutes, though it is more like 30 seconds in earthly time. I am feeling in awe and sensing pure love as this is happening. When I feel the speed of the words slowing down, I back away a bit, but then the words come at me stronger as if to say, "Hold on - you don't have all the answers yet." So, I lean in until there are no more.

At this point, the face of my beloved, deceased mother appears to me. She says nothing, but she smiles with a deep sense of approval. We embrace for a long time (I feel her embrace, though I never see her body). I can feel the tears flowing down my 3D body as I sit in the hypnosis chair, yet I am still in that room with the cedar chest, embracing my mother.

The facilitator asked me if my mother had a message for me. What do I need to know?

The message from my mother is, "You are enough."

Her love is so intense and complete, so I seal that love by placing my hands upon my heart. I never want to lose that feeling. I received another message, though not from my mother. It is the word TRUST. I believe it came from a higher source. The moments go by, and I begin to feel very full.

As the session concludes, I feel there is nothing else I need to know right now in order to transform and to go forward with absolute knowingness, assuredness, and confidence. I feel so loved and so complete.

I am guided back down the silver cord to my Happy, Safe Place in the woods. I take a few moments there to feel this tremendous sense of peace. I have found it so interesting that you can be there and be here at the same time. I could be fully in a trance, having this wild experience, yet I could feel the warmth of the tears as they ran down my physical, 3D face. I was not unconscious or oblivious to the facilitator's existence in the room, yet I was not concerned in any way. I was fully in the experience with my Higher-Self.

For a few days after that quantum journey, I felt an overwhelming sense of love and peace. I was so calm. Nothing bothered me. I found myself reflecting on the experience for weeks afterward. What has changed for me? Well, besides having all the answers (ha!), I don't have any fear or anxiety related to the questions I had coming into the session. My sense of trust has definitely increased. I'm accepting things as they unfold. And, just maybe, I'm asking better questions.

This journey is such a beautiful example of how the subconscious communicates in ways that feel both symbolic and deeply personal. The hallway, the silver cord, the totem pole, the tunnel—all of these are the mind's way of translating profound inner wisdom into imagery the conscious mind can grasp. What might look random at first often carries meaning that continues to unfold long after the session.

I especially love the moment when the client opened the cedar chest and found not just one answer, but a stream of them flowing directly into their mind and body. This is what happens when we stop searching outside of ourselves and let the deeper layers of consciousness provide what we've been craving—clarity, direction, and peace.

The embrace from their mother and the message "You are enough" is one of those experiences that bypasses logic entirely. You can study hypnosis for years, but when you feel something that real, that loving, that embodied, you realize the subconscious isn't "pretending." It's revealing.

And perhaps the most practical takeaway here is this: the client didn't come out of the session with every step of their future mapped out. Instead, they came out with something even more powerful—the felt sense of trust. *That shift alone often transforms how we show up, make decisions, and allow abundance to flow more naturally.*

~Kryssa

My Experience in the Akashic Records

By Robyn Monteleone

As far as the Akashic Records were concerned, I was a complete novice. I had heard the name. I did not have a concept of what the Akashic Records were. I had done no reading, no study. I had no frame of reference; I had no expectations. I came into the QJH session with a particular goal, though I had no expectations as to how to achieve my goal. The unfolding of the journey was part of its enchantment.

The first thing that was different for me was that my happy, safe place became a surreal place I had never been to before. I became immersed in a beautiful, serene, and breathtaking scene that seemed to be part of the Northern Lights. I wasn't on land. I was somehow immersed in the atmosphere, in the streams of coloured light surrounding me, enveloping me, holding me safe. A beautiful, otherworldly place where I was simply part of the swirling atmosphere. The jump forward was a small one from here.

After some preliminary work, the suggestion was given to visit the Akashic Records. The doorway turned out to be a long distance away, with twists and turns, and the journey took some time. It was the last door, the furthest door away in the Hallway of Answers. The door was magnificent. A glittering mass of pink and blue crystals, similar to breaking open a geode and finding the crystal mass inside with all its gradations. Glowing, sparkling with crystals, gems, and diamonds.

I instinctively felt this was not a door to simply rush through. This was a door that needed due reverence. First, I needed to bow and then ask permission to enter. The Souls communed and granted us (my hypnotherapist, Kryssa, and I) permission to enter.

I entered a cathedral-like space and found a single book on a pedestal. The book was open. The pages were blank, and under advice, I put my hands on the book. It didn't seem quite right, so I then hovered my hands above the book. The light was initially too much, and I needed help to adjust to its power.

I was called to bring "The Family" forward. The Family was a group of souls, not a family in the human sense. Beings that were called on to be connected to me. Their role is to provide support and communicate with me, using their hive mind. Surrounded by their support, I was able to begin to access data from the Akashic Records and received information on my lifespan and other information.

My earthly family was then called in so I could 'negotiate' with them to be 'bigger' and to work towards my dreams. 'Permission' was sought. My energetic husband simply asked for more communication (a fair request). My energetic in-laws and mother found it difficult to understand why I was seeking 'permission' to work towards my dreams, as they didn't feel the need for me to be anything more than what I was. Their energies were heavy, so they were bathed in light. My energetic children were given their own wings to fly and fulfill their own dreams.

I use the word permission simply because this is the word I used during the session. As I write this, my conscious, logical mind is almost offended that I needed to negotiate and ask permission from my earthly family to work towards my goals and to seek a life bigger than it was at the time. Particularly, the family I am negotiating with consists of parents and in-laws who live separately and have no bearing on my finances and day-to-day decisions. Regardless, this permission was sought.

Much of this experience was beyond my conscious awareness and could not be recorded. The 'negotiations' with my family took time, and I have no awareness of what happened in that realm. I can only assume the negotiations concluded and that I was able to receive information from the Akashic Records. I felt my hands begin to twitch, and then my arms began to lift slowly. Over several minutes, my arms rose up until my arms were at shoulder height. My arms then changed direction and began to move until my fingers clasped and then lay across my heart. I felt my chest expand as I breathed more deeply.

I felt like I had been given a most precious gift, although I didn't know what it was.

I was given the 'to shine'.

I have little conscious awareness of what I downloaded from the Akashic Records. However, I could physically feel the download being received.

Follow-up thoughts.

This session occurred during a time when I had a lot of family obligations impacting my time and ability to dedicate myself to working towards my dream of building up my hypnotherapy practice. In the following days and weeks, I felt a sense of urgency to make decisions and finalize a family matter that had become outstanding. A matter I had pushed to the side for several months as I dealt with other matters that were more urgent. I spent the next 12 months working on this task that I didn't want to do but needed to.

Having finished this mammoth task, and after giving myself time to rest, I had more time, energy, and focus to put towards my goals, and I felt energy flowing, so I could move forward. I am now moving in the direction I want to move in. I don't feel like I'm fighting against invisible forces now. Now, I feel I am free and supported to keep moving in the direction that I have chosen.

What I love about this session is that it shows how little *prior knowledge someone needs in order to access profound wisdom. This client had never studied the Akashic Records, never read about them, and yet their subconscious mind led them straight into an experience rich with reverence, imagery, and information. To me, that's one of the most validating aspects of Quantum Journeys Hypnosis™—people don't have to know the "right" symbols or scripts ahead of time. The wisdom emerges spontaneously, in a way that feels deeply personal.*

This journey was also the inspiration for the Akashic Records module inside QJHA. The crystalline door, the sense of asking permission before entering, and the download that came in the form of a physical, felt shift—these became part of the framework I now teach students for helping clients access the Records responsibly and with reverence.

The client later became a QJHA graduate, which makes this one even more meaningful. They went from experiencing the Records for the first time, wide-eyed and open-hearted, to guiding others through that same sacred doorway. To me, that's the beauty of this work: one person's journey often plants the seed for a collective pathway forward.

~Kryssa

Healing the Witch Wound

By Carolyn Mather

I wanted to work through blocks holding me back in my new hypnotherapy business, but I have been on a more spiritual path as well, and in the lead-up to my session, things had been happening that I felt were 'signs' that I also needed to pursue that. Things such as seeing the word 'which' misspelt as 'witch' multiple times, black cats turning up in my garden and even coming into my house, pulling an oracle card in a women's group with the word 'witch', (the group being where I first heard the concept of 'the witch wound') and having strange snapshot 'memories' of being drowned in a pond. I was also told in a reading with a medium that doubts about my own spiritual abilities are because I would have been persecuted in a past life for them. As well as numerous other symbols and synchronicities. Just before the session with Kryssa started, she exclaimed that there was a hummingbird outside the window. I'd heard someone mention on a podcast a few days before that this was a good omen for something, but they weren't sure what.

During the session, we discussed goals to release my fears and blocks around my new business. I had newly set up in practice doing QJH myself and was loving it, but also felt something was getting in the way. I had been brave enough to put myself out there, but I still had some fears, which led me to question my abilities and whether I was on the right path. We also agreed we would ask my Higher-Self whether a more spiritual route was in my highest good.

During the induction, the healing light made me feel illuminated like a shining star; it was electric, and I already began to feel a shift. I went to my happy, safe place, which was a beautiful garden with little birds and flowers with the most incredible colors. I went to sleep in a pink cocoon and then went on a transformational journey. I'd been to the hallway of answers before, but this time it had crystals as well as flowers, colored doors with stained glass, and a sky with multi-colored stars. We looked for a door to meet my Higher-Self. It was bright pink with angels in a stained-glass window.

We met with my Higher-Self, whom I've met before and come to know well, but also two angels were there. I didn't know their names at first, but they stayed with us for the journey. Kryssa asked, Do I have a connection to the angelic realm. My Higher-

Self said yes. When asked what the connection is, my Higher-Self said they are calling me to do this work. We asked will they would be there for her, as she does this work, and she said yes. Kryssa then asked does she had anything to be afraid of, given that she had angels supporting her. My Higher-Self said no.

Kryssa asked what can we could do, so I could really grasp that. The answer from my Higher-Self was to talk to them more. We asked how I could communicate better with the angels. My Higher-Self said Just ask. When asked how I could be sure they were answering, my Higher-Self said she needed to know it was them, not her imagination, she had been feeling tingling in her hands and feet, like sparks (which I had been feeling since working on my connection to the spirit world), and she would feel that and know it's them. Kryssa asked if the angels could give me that feeling now, in the session, and they did.

My Higher-Self told me I was on the right path because angels were calling me to it. She also told me that mediumship is something that I would be good at. We asked if it is in my highest good to increase my mediumship skills, which my Higher-Self agreed to do, but just a little for now, as too much would be overwhelming, and I can then continue to develop from there. For a few weeks prior to the session, I had been practicing spirit connection and dialing this up and down on 'radio dials'. She said that she would put notches and numbers on the dials, so that I could be more precise, rather than just spinning them around. We asked what else would help, and she said just trust in what is happening- trust that it is a spirit connection and not just imagination. We asked how I could know this. She said I will feel that same tingling energy in my feet and hands and know it is spirit.

We asked about what was blocking me, my Higher-Self said she had been punished before, she was punished for being a witch. Kryssa asked if I needed to go there now or if my Higher-Self just cleared it. She said I needed to go there, and I was ready to go there. We were asked to go to whatever lifetime we need to explore to understand where this comes from, for me to address it.

I found a black door and went through it. I was in a dark, small, enclosed forest- the same one from my snapshot memories. It was nighttime, with a small, dark, murky, overgrown pond. I was guided to look down from the point of view of the departed soul and walk through what was happening. I saw myself being taken slowly and silently to the pond and put into the water. It was my own family that took me there. They put me into the water, but it was controlled and gentle, not brutal. They held my head under the water, just calmly and quietly in the dark. It was somehow peaceful how they did it. I was asked what year it was; I don't know why, but 1612 came to mind. I was asked where I was, and Yorkshire came to my mind.

I (in this lifetime) was crying and trembling, with powerful emotion. I was guided to look at it happening from above, and Kryssa asked why I thought my family had done it. I could see that they were just confused and scared. They were saving me from someone else doing it. And what they did was gentler than what would have been done to me by others. I was able to see that it was like a mercy killing. Kryssa asked why I think my family did it. I said because I was a witch. She asked if I was really a witch? Why did they think that? What was I really doing? It was because I used herbs and potions to heal people. And I could talk to spirits. I didn't understand it, I was only young, but I couldn't help myself doing it, I was drawn to it. People found out. The family didn't explain why they were doing it to me at the time, but they were scared of what would happen to me. I was then guided to let this lifetime reach its end.

Kryssa asked the little girl her name. It was Selina. She guided her to rise up, rejoin, and integrate with her soul. Kryssa asked if it was in my highest good to bring forth those skills of Selina's to this lifetime. My Higher-Self said yes. Kryssa asked what Selina would think if she could see the world now. Imagine how much different life would be for her if things had been widely accepted. With so many people doing the work. I said Selina would say 'Lucky you'. You can tell people what you do, go on the internet, read about it, learn about it, and talk to like-minded people. Kryssa asked, Can we bring forth the skills to this life, and use them with intention instead of accidentally? So, she can continue to do this work without fear of persecution? So, she can be proud. My Higher-Self said yes.

Kryssa asked if I could forgive my family. I could understand they were just scared and didn't know what to do. They were terrified of being bullied. I was guided to release the trauma, knowing that I could keep the wisdom, skills, and talents and allow them to continue to develop. I was encouraged to bring them to right here, right now, amplifying the ability, enjoying the sense of liberation, knowing I can do it without fear.

We asked my Higher-Self to expand my heart space so that I can feel it in my heart, and when a potential client who is aligned with me makes contact, I will know. She agreed to do this, and I felt the warmth and love expanding. We asked my Higher-Self what percentage of consciousness I have in this lifetime. It was 40. She agreed to increase this to 60, gently and in my own time, so as not to be overwhelming. We asked for advice for my business. She said I need help from others for practical things like marketing and a website. But otherwise, 'just be you'. The people you want to work with are sensitive and will know if you're not being authentic. And you need to be yourself to be able to help them in the way you need to. That's what you're here to do. It will all come together and work in combination: hypnosis, mediumship, and card reading. I had become drawn to spirit release therapy, but my Higher-Self said that it wasn't for me. She said I was drawn to it because I needed my own clearing done (which I had a few weeks prior to the session, and it was highly beneficial), but that spirit release work is too dark for me. I need to work in love and light, doing one-to-one readings for people with their loved ones in spirit. She said I am a light worker.

My Higher-Self also told me to wear pink and more turquoise.

In the end, I recognized the two angels as Raphael and Aurora. Kryssa said she had met them a few times. I had met Raphael before, too, not Aurora, but I realised she's always been there. Kryssa said I could reach out and hug them if I wanted. But it was Angel Raphael who reached out to hug me. It was the most powerful, beautiful feeling of love and warmth; I could feel his energy and angel wings around me. I knew that I was loved and protected and on the right path. And that I wanted to do Selina proud.

After the session, I looked up 1612.

It was the date of the Pendle witch trials, which I have heard of but wouldn't have consciously remembered the date if you'd asked me.

I also looked up what it means to see a hummingbird:

Challenging times are over, and healing can begin.

Good luck, or a loved one's spirit is with you.

Some sessions unfold in a way that feels like a deep remembering—not just for the client, but for me as the facilitator too. This journey carried the unmistakable energy of both initiation and reclamation. What stood out most was how gracefully her Higher-self orchestrated the experience: showing her the fears, connecting them to the "witch wound," and then weaving those threads forward into empowerment, authenticity, and spiritual service.

This client later shared with me that she has since stepped fully into a career as a professional medium. To witness someone go from uncertainty and self-doubt to hearing, "You are a light worker," and then living into that truth—that is why I do this work. These sessions don't just bring healing; they often reveal a calling. And sometimes, the courage to embrace that calling is exactly what transforms not only a client's life, but also the lives of the people they're here to serve.

~Kryssa

Wounded and Lonely Ego State Befriends Entity Attachments

By Kryssa Marie Bowman

I have quite a bit of childhood trauma that I've been processing, working through, and healing from for most of my life. And all things considered, I'm doing a pretty good job of it if I do say so myself. However, there is one wounded child state that has been resistant to changing or evolving or doing things differently because she believes she saved my life when I was 13 years old. And she's not wrong.

She wouldn't come to the surface- or what people in the field would call "the executive state" -very often, but when she did, she would wreak absolute havoc on my life! She was very destructive and high-risk. She was the part that helped me escape after a particularly traumatizing event when I was 13 years old. She later prompted me to run away to New York City at age 15. She has terrible taste in partners, and she is a master at self-sabotage.

Whenever things were going really well in my life, she would be lurking just around the corner waiting to pull the proverbial rug out from beneath my feet and leave everything in ruins. You might be thinking that she, herself, was an entity attachment based on this behavior. But no, she was an honest-to-goodness part of me...and I'm still alive partially because of her.

In her own way, she believed she was helping me. She was afraid that when things were going too well for me, someone would take notice and cause me harm. She was afraid that if I became successful, I would become a target. If I were too attractive, too smart, too popular, too anything that would cause others to notice me, then I would be in harm's way. She felt it was her job to jump in and sabotage me whenever I might get too close to the spotlight.

Obviously, a person can't live like that, but historically, she was really resistant to changing. She might do a little bit, but it was more to get me to stop pestering her and just let her be because, in her perception, the fact that I was still alive was proof that she was doing a fantastic job of protecting me! But one day, when I could sense that I was just about to blow up my life- precisely because everything was working so well- I decided to go into trance and have a little chat with her.

She was bedraggled, dirty, and angry, and presented herself to me like an adolescent punk rock girlie. I told her I liked her look, which caught her by surprise. I asked her if she was aware that I'm 54 now, not 13 or 15. She had not realized this. I asked if she thought she was doing a good job protecting me, and she said yes, so I proceeded to show her the wreckage and devastation she left in the aftermath of her "protection", and I told her that I'd grown out of needing that kind of help. That the kind of help she was providing was, in fact, causing me and my family great harm.

She was surprised and also apologetic. When it came time to help her evolve, she revealed to me that she wasn't alone. That she had picked up a few friends in the form of lost soul entity attachments to keep her company since she wasn't welcome to be with my other ego/resource states. They disliked her. (Which of course fed into her victim complex). So, in order to help her, I had to first help these lost souls move on to the rest of their souls' journey. This was my first introduction to the concept that a subconscious part, or ego state, could intentionally attract entities.

Uncovering the Roots of Unexplained Sadness

By Igor Vilusic

Have you ever felt sadness wash over you for no apparent reason? A distinct feeling of melancholy that seems misplaced in an otherwise joyful setting? I experienced this peculiar sensation at family celebrations throughout my life. While loved ones laughed and bonded, I struggled with an unexplainable grief. This persistent feeling led me on a journey to uncover its origins.

I decided to undergo past life regression to see if this sorrow originated in a previous lifetime. Eleven years ago, I decided to have a spiritual hypnosis session and experience my past lives. For many years of my life, I felt strange and uneasy. When I would sit in family gatherings, whether for birthdays, celebrations, or regular dinners, a feeling would often come up—a feeling that was foreign, a feeling that wasn't mine, a feeling that made me feel sad, a feeling that pulled me out of that experience of engaging with my family, with loved ones, having a meal, laughing, and sharing stories.

My mind would pull me out of that experience, and I felt as if I didn't belong there, as if something was wrong, or something didn't feel quite right. Occasionally, people around me would ask, "Are you okay?", "What's going on?" But most of the time, nobody would notice anything, and I would ignore that feeling.

But through the years, that feeling got stronger and stronger. So, I went on a quest to determine what this is, where it comes from, and what it wants. I've researched many things, but something was pulling me to experience my past life, and that's something people call God. Their will, their intuition, and many other words. I call it inner guidance.

My inner guidance was always more robust and led me to discover many new things.

This time, my inner guidance pulled me to experience this. But my mind wasn't quite ready, and I had a lot of resistance to it because it involved a different person. It evolved into a practitioner. It meant I would have to open up and share my feelings.

So, one morning, I sat down in my car and drove for hours. Took me around 5 hours to finally arrive at my destination. I had an intense conversation with myself.

"Why do I want to do this?"

"How do I know that I can experience it?"

"How do I know if it's real? How do I know if I can trust the practitioner?"

"Hell, can I even trust myself?"

My inner guidance kept me driving, kept me moving forward, and I trusted it and leaned on it because most of the time, I exhaust myself from thinking, analyzing, and judging.

My inner guidance has a light energy, doesn't talk much, and it's sure.

So, finally, I arrived. I was a little bit nervous. I wasn't quite sure if I would go forward, but I kept going, taking the next stage. The session started with the practitioner asking me a lot of questions. I wondered, *'Why are you asking so many questions? Why are you so nosy? Why do you want to know everything'?*

I had to laugh to myself. I wouldn't show it to her. I knew why I was here.

I answered that I wanted to experience a past-life regression. I've heard many stories about it and find it interesting. While that was true, that's not why I was there. I was there because I had feelings that made me sad, apparently for no particular reason or one that I didn't know to me. So, I continued answering questions truthfully, and the rest I kept to myself.

The practitioner brought me into a different room where I would have the experience. So, I lay down on the couch, she gave me a blanket, and she guided me into a nice, relaxed Kipnu state. But my mind was alert, and I was controlling and questioning every word that she was saying and how she was saying it. My inner guidance wanted to have that experience or wanted me to experience it.

She guided me into a beautiful green garden like an early spring garden. There were flowers, bright colors, sunlight, trees, and a wall of stones that was so long that when I looked at it, there was no end to it. On those walls, there were doors, and each door represented a lifetime. Again, my inner guidance was asked, "Which one do you feel pulled towards?"

Looking at all of these doors, I looked at them, and I chose one that beckoned me closer and closer. As I touched the door handle, that wooden door opened. I felt pulled into a different world. The hands that pulled that wooden door, opened it, and stepped into it were now those of a young boy. He was merely five or six. He had a problem turning the door handle, and he opened it up and went into the kitchen. In the kitchen was his mother.

The practitioner asked me, "What do you see? What are you experiencing? What's the sense that you're getting?"

"My mother was cooking something." She smiled at me, and I smiled at her.

When I looked around the kitchen, everything was made out of wood. It was centuries ago. I wasn't quite sure what year it was. It felt like the 16th century. We were living on a farm. We had that house, a simple house. I went outside. There were animals, and my father was coming back from work. He's been working all day, working in the field. We also had our own vegetables and animals. Suddenly, we jumped later into this lifetime into the following significant scene.

I was older. I was almost 18 or 19. The area where we lived was like a village. I had dreams. I wanted to go see the world and go to bigger cities. I didn't like being on the farm and working in the field, but that's what I have been doing with my father my whole life. And then my father got a little bit sick, and as a result, I was forced to work more. That longing to go somewhere became a distant wish. It felt like a different lifetime, something that I couldn't do.

A year passed, and then another one, and another one, and another one. Inside, I was dying slowly and fast-forwarding to the next crucial or significant event in that lifetime.

There wasn't any. My parents had died. I'm still that far away, living alone. I worked in the field, and this was how life went on and on. The possibilities at that stage of my life, I don't even see any hope. I only see fear.

Fast-forward to the last five minutes before I die in this lifetime. Looking back over that lifetime, what were the life lessons? What did I learn? My life started hopefully, with a loving family. However, as the years passed by, I couldn't follow my dream. The sad part is that I don't even remember what the dream was. The only thing that I do know and remember is the regret of not going out into the world, exploring the world, and looking for the life that I wanted to live. I lived a life on somebody else's terms, but I wasn't quite sure what the reason for it was, and as I let go of that life, I was back in that beautiful spring garden.

The sound of nature created a symphony. I felt the warmth of the sun and the birds in the background, heard the summer breeze, and the gentle movement of sand. Looking at that wall, that endless wall of stones or doors. A new door appeared, which was my new life that I wanted to explore. I felt the pull. Three, two, one, click and go towards it. So, I went with my inner guidance. As I touched the door handle and opened the door, I smiled as I stepped into this new lifetime. It looked to be about the eighteen hundreds.

I had a smile on my face in that lifetime. I was a woman. I was a tall, beautiful woman, an attractive one. I saw how other people were looking at my body. I had long hair and long curls, and I felt good. I was working. I worked in a bar. I loved that job. I loved being surrounded by people. I joked that I entertained, and I earned great money.

But one day, someone came in. A man. I felt different. There was a spark, there was chemistry, but I didn't let it show. I didn't give a signal. He felt it, too. As he looked at me, I ignored him. Then, when he looked or talked to somebody else, I'd glance at him.

It didn't feel good. It feels special. I'd never felt like that before. When I asked myself, why haven't I given a signal? Why haven't I said something? It felt like I didn't deserve that kind of love or attention. That man was remarkable. I knew it. Usually, I would get hit on by customers, but I wasn't interested in them at all. I was rather repelled and disgusted. But this one is different.

He waited a few hours for me, but I never came over. Ignored him, and he went.

And from that day on, things changed. Days, months, and years passed, and I was hoping to see him again. I dreamed of being with him, of having a family with him. But he wasn't there. He didn't come. He never came. So, I couldn't keep working. I changed jobs. Years passed.

In the next scene, I am older, and I don't have anyone. I'm reading books.

I'm taking care of older people who are sick. I basically live with them until they pass away. Then, I take care of a new person, as there isn't much to do because these people are in pain. I read books all the time. Sitting on that wooden chair, reading books, and feeling that empty feeling, I recognize it. I was unfortunate that I didn't say anything, that I didn't give a signal. I was heartbroken.

I broke my own heart. I'd never given somebody a chance to break my heart, and going forward to the last five minutes before I die, I regretted my life and the choices that I made of not giving love a chance, of not allowing myself to be loved and hurt, or maybe not, but to experience that deep connection. This second life was somewhere in Scandinavia.

As the practitioner guided me back to this beautiful spring garden, I could smell the flowers and breathe again, lighter. But that life experience was heavy. It was a burden, and I recognized that feeling in my life. That woman, it was her feelings. It's her deep sadness that I felt when I was at family gatherings, when there was no need to feel it. It's her, right? At that moment, I felt relieved that I could relate to the woman's feelings, that I was in a second life that I had just experienced.

The practitioner asked me, "What's next door calling you?"

I was exhausted, but another one was calling me. I was going faster towards it. I don't know why, but I was just following my inner guidance. I opened the door, and immediately, everything changed again.

I felt as if I was in a cowboy movie or somewhere in America, somewhere in the south, there was a guy, a young guy. We were a group of five, a true brotherhood. We did everything together. And when I mean everything, I mean everything, we were robbing bars. Actually, anything that we could rob, get on our horses, and ride to the next village to spend it on women and alcohol. I looked forward to that life, but it only lasted for a couple of years, until one morning, our luck turned.

We planned to rob something more significant because we were tired of constantly needing to. We did not want to work so much. We never killed anyone, but we did threaten people. One day, we went into this small town, and I wanted to rob. I wasn't quite sure what that was. It was sort of like a shop. We had always had a plan, but that morning, things turned. Out of these five guys, I had one who was my closest friend. He was like my brother. I didn't have any family. I had parents, but I don't even know where they lived or what they did. I could count on him in every situation. My name was James. As we tried to rob the shop, my best friend was shot.

We tried to help him, put him on the horse, and get him out of there, but it was too late. He died then and there. That was the moment that I radically changed my life. I left the group, I left my brotherhood, and I went to a bar and saw a waitress, and I thought to myself, I'm gonna get a job, I'm gonna settle down, and I'm gonna change my life. So, I did; it was as if I had never been part of that group, my brotherhood, and what we had done. I completely changed my life.

I got myself a job, and I worked, and that waitress became my wife, and we created a family with a couple of kids together. Fast forward to the last five minutes of my life as I reviewed it. I was happy. I was happy that I made the decision. I missed my brother, but I wouldn't have changed without him. And who knows how my life would have ended.

I was deeply thankful for him.

As I let go of that life, of that third life experience on that field, an older man and a young girl appeared. The girl was playful, bubbly, curious, hopeful, and cheerful, and she asked a lot of questions. That older man looked really old but wise. He didn't speak much, but when he did, you could feel that it had some importance and significance, and that's the power dynamic that I experienced within me. There is that playful, fun, joyful, sometimes even naive, and light-hearted energy that I had, and then there's a deep knowledge and wisdom that resides within me, balancing that female energy with the masculine energy.

It was an exciting journey for me. There were times in my life when the young girl guide led, and there were times when the old and wise man took over; it was as if two people resided in me, two different energies. Getting to know them a little bit helped me understand myself more and learn about the qualities I had access to. It's not either or, but it's both, and I get to choose when I need it.

The practitioner then guided me into a different scenario in which I was me in this lifetime, fully dressed. However, I was taking off my clothes. I was a little bit nervous.

I needed to go into a lovely river. Inessa was taking every step and getting closer to the river, and I felt liberated. I felt open, and with each step, I was getting deeper into the water until I could swim. So, I took a deep breath and went under the water.

As I went under the water, I felt like an energy field around me—some call it aura—was being pulled up like layers and layers on top of them. Each moment I was underwater, swimming, and moving my hands, I felt energy being liberated, as if I was being released and relieved and letting go of suffering, pain, and any unnecessary emotion. And with each layer that was removed, my aura was being liberated. I felt strong. I never felt so strong in my life. My body felt never so strong. The strength I felt in my physical body was out of this world. My body was taking a different shape. I had become more muscular. I was strong physically and mentally. I was liberated. I was at peace and could relax after a very long time.

As I came out of the water, out of that river, and stepped onto the ground, onto earth, man, I felt powerful. I could feel in every cell how strong I was, how powerful it felt to be in my body, a filtered peace. And that inner guidance brought me a certainty I hadn't experienced before, and I stayed in that moment. I loved being that person. I loved noticing how it felt within that muscular body.

The practitioner guided me out of that whole experience back into my life. I stayed lying there for a couple more minutes, and then we went into the other room to talk about my experience and what I had learned. Again, I saw myself not sharing. I didn't want it to be shared. I told her a couple of things, but merely 30% of what I had experienced. I wanted to keep that experience for myself.

But one thing I was sure of was the sadness that I was feeling when we would gather around holidays, birthdays, and family meetings. I knew the deep sadness that I was feeling wasn't mine. I knew that I didn't have anything to do with it in this lifetime, in my lifetime, but I knew who it belonged to. I learned to acknowledge it, and I understood it as a wake-up call to give love a chance. And I did. In this lifetime, I did. I opened my heart a couple of times and let my heart experience all the faces of love. I could experience what it was like to be in love, to love someone, and to lose someone. I never knew my heart could love this profoundly.

This session changed me in many different ways. It allowed me to follow my dreams even though I didn't feel I was ready or deserving, or did not know where that would lead me. So many of my so-called accomplishments in this lifetime result from that session.

Was I still feeling fearful from time to time? You bet I do. But you know what else I learned? I learned that I needed to cultivate and awaken the courage to stay with the fear. Let the fear be there and still go after what I want. My inner guidance would always pull me forward. I leaned on it and trusted it; it has enriched my life in every shape and form.

Today, this is the reason why I help humans go deep inside and look for answers and lessons to create a life that is only imaginable to them.

Courage is calling.

Do you hear it? Are you ready to answer?

What I love most about this story is how clearly it shows the way unexplained emotions in our present life can often be echoes from somewhere else. *The client began with an ache of sadness that didn't seem to belong in their current life. Through regression, that heaviness was revealed as the residue of other lifetimes—lives filled with regret, with missed opportunities, with unspoken love.*

And here's the beauty: once the subconscious connects the dots, that misplaced sorrow no longer runs the show. It transforms from an invisible weight into a teacher. This client walked away with clarity that the sadness they carried wasn't theirs alone, and even more importantly, with permission to live differently this time. To follow dreams, to open the heart, to let love in.

Sessions like this remind us that hypnosis isn't about escaping reality—it's about reclaiming it. When we meet the echoes of other times and bring them into the light, we don't just heal the past—we change how we live today.

~Kryssa

My Twin Flame Quantum Journey

By Sreshtha Tewari

My Twin Flame is smiling at me. His smile is filled with so much admiration, joy, and love. This visualization has stayed with me since my session with Kryssa earlier this month. I can still see it plainly.

My name is Sreshtha Tewari, and I'm an Emotional Intelligence Love Coach. I won a session with Kryssa through my attendance at the Hypnothoughts Live! Conference. I didn't really understand what the session was about or what I had won. However, when Kryssa started to ask me questions, my love life came up.

I don't like talking about my love life one-on-one. It is something that feels extremely vulnerable to me. When I teach and tell my stories, it is always on my terms, and I am the one directing the conversation.

In my first meeting with Kryssa, she told me to just answer what came first. She asked, "What would you like to treat?" The answer automatically came: "Underlying sadness." She then asked, "What do you hope to gain?" I answered, "Understanding." This was followed by, "What would you like to understand?"—and without knowing why I was saying it, I answered, "True love." I shocked myself because I never speak about this one-on-one. However, when Kryssa explained the journey to the Hallway of Answers, I became excited.

I had been on a Twin Flame journey for most of my life without knowing it. I only recognized who my Twin Flame was two years ago. That recognition led me on the path of understanding my own life and becoming a Love Coach. While I had gained a lot of understanding, I still didn't fully comprehend much of it.

If you are reading this and don't know what a Twin Flame is, let me explain. A Twin Flame is the same soul split into two. As such, you carry the same exact soul frequency or soul song. This is different from a soulmate, as a soulmate vibrates close to—but not exactly on—your frequency. A soulmate can also be platonic, e.g., a mother, sister, or friend.

Twin Flames usually meet, share a deep connection (not necessarily sexual, but deeply emotional and romantic) for three to six months. After this, one party suddenly breaks it off, plunging the other into unexplainable, deep turmoil. I have been in this state for more than 20 years, consistently believing I will never be good enough for him.

While the prospect of going into the Hallway of Answers was exciting, it was also terrifying for me. I had known about past life regression since the late '90s. I have read all of Dr. Brian Weiss's books and attended two of his workshops. However, I never wanted to regress to figure out my love story, because I did not want to see my love with the person he chose over me in this life, either in regression or in the present. I was definitely scared I would see that.

Nevertheless, as I had won this session, I trusted in its timing and presence in my life.

In the beginning, Kryssa took me to a cloud to rest my analytical mind. I felt extremely comfortable and relaxed. The next thing I remember is going into the Hallway of Answers.

I didn't quite see a hallway. I was up in the sky, standing in the center of reels of film circling around me. It was like a long reel of negative film with still pictures. Kryssa suggested I choose or go into one.

On that suggestion, I saw Jesus hand me a scene. It was a beautiful scene with the bluest sky. There was a hot-air balloon in the background, green grass, and my Twin Flame. He had the brightest smile on his face and was beckoning me to come into the scene with him. Kryssa asked me what lifetime it was, and the answer I got was: this lifetime. Then she asked what year it was—the answer I got was 1974. This was interesting, as it is actually the year of his birth.

I was a bit confused because in the vision, he was an adult, but I knew he would have been a baby in 1974. She advised me not to worry about time—that it's not necessarily in the order we believe. He kept calling me into the scene, but I didn't want to go in.

The next thing I knew, I suddenly began crying vehemently. All the underlying sadness had surfaced. I couldn't control or stop the crying. On Kryssa's prompt, the reason came: I didn't want to come into this life—it was my Twin Flame who wanted me to come into this life with him.

I had always known I didn't want to come into this life. My mother used to tell me I didn't want to be born, as they literally had to pull me out of her. However, knowing that my Twin Flame was the one who beckoned me to come made me so incredibly sad, given everything I had experienced on my Twin Flame journey. I initially thought we both decided to come to experience the separation. However, knowing that this was his creation felt like being stabbed and betrayed all over again.

The funny thing is, I actually had a vision of this one month before, but I didn't know what it was. I was sitting in a class with Anand Rao, following one of his meditations. In that meditation, I saw both my Twin Flame and myself emerging from an extremely bright light. We were dressed in robes—my Twin Flame was in royal blue and I was in purple. He was running and pulling me with him. We ran faster and faster. He kept pulling me until we started to roll, but he went ahead of me.

Kryssa then suggested we go back to the signing of the Earth contract, as I was still crying. I was immediately plunged into darkness. I eventually saw myself as a baby, with God and my Twin Flame in his royal blue robe. I saw them both tending to me and comforting me as I was being born. I still didn't want to be here after birth, and I felt they were both comforting me.

Kryssa told me to ask why I came into this lifetime to experience the separation. The answer I got was: for the love to be even sweeter. When I got this answer, I saw both my Twin Flame and myself swirling upward, entwining with each other in blue and purple.

She also asked how many lifetimes we had been together. The answer that came was "beyond time." The final thing she asked was: What is the lesson in this lifetime? The answer I heard was "eternal love." Some part of me always knew these answers; however, marrying them with the depth of pain and emotion I felt was challenging.

We also asked about reunion in this lifetime, because I felt close to it, as I know he is currently going through an "awakening." I received an answer that it was happening soon, which was comforting. In the visualization, he explained that he had to leave his current relationship in the most peaceful way, which I certainly appreciated.

I also inquired about my career, as at this time, I still had my corporate job. The overwhelming message was that everyone was supporting and guiding me. I saw several people with whom I currently work clapping for me and cheering me on. The message was that I needed to enjoy every moment at work and with the people I meet.

This was valuable to me, as I had been slowly detaching myself from that environment due to constant disappointment. However, since then I have changed my mentality and try my best to enjoy being in the environment and interacting with others. I also got a clear message to attend an upcoming function I had previously decided not to attend.

In the end, all my guides came in. I saw my grandparents, my aunt, and many others. One of my friends, who also currently guides me spiritually, appeared, reminding me how loved I am. I also saw my Twin Flame return at the end, telling me, "I love you so much," beaming with love—and of course, his smile. I felt consoled.

As we were closing, I saw my higher-self high up in the sky. She was completely radiant and beautiful. She showered me with an extraordinary amount of golden light. I felt instantly calm and filled with love. I don't think I can do justice to this part of the vision—it was completely amazing.

On coming back to reality, I felt an amazing calm and peace. It was almost stillness. At that time, I had still been listening to nighttime meditations to help with my self-esteem. I suddenly felt I didn't need to do that anymore. In fact, I felt I needed to do nothing. All I had to do was "just be." Having followed so many people who teach manifestation, I had heard this message before, but never understood it until now.

My life completely changed, and I entered the "knowing state." The knowing state is when you let go of all doubt or worry, with no question that your wishes are coming true.

Even though I left the session feeling absolutely fantastic, the message about my Twin Flame "making me come" into this life because he wanted me to plagued me. That sadness lingered for days.

I prayed about it, and eventually I realized one of my lessons was to trust his intentions. I had to trust that he knows what is best for us. I had to trust in his vision and creation of this life for us. Most of all, I had to trust that he is cheering for our reunion as much as I am. As I sink into that trust, I continue to see him smiling at me.

My appreciation for this experience is infinite.

What stands out to me here is how hypnosis allows us to meet the heart where it already lives—in symbols, visions, and felt truths. Whether or not you resonate with the concept of Twin Flames, the transformation isn't about labels. It's about what the experience unlocked for this client: a sense of peace, trust, and clarity that reshaped how she moves through her life.

In sessions like these, my role isn't to confirm or deny anyone's beliefs. It's to hold the space where the subconscious can reveal what it needs to—whether that looks like a soul contract, a radiant guide, or simply the feeling of finally being loved and safe. When the nervous system feels that shift, it doesn't just stay in the imagination. It ripples into daily life, quieting doubts, softening old wounds, and opening the way for new ways of being.

For this client, the takeaway was learning to rest in the "knowing state"—where trust replaces fear, and being replaces striving. That's the real gift of this work: not answers that come from me, but answers that rise from within them.

~Kryssa

Epilogue: The Future Is Quantum

In a world where both the spiritual and the scientific are vying to explain the mysteries of existence, perhaps our greatest awakening comes when we stop choosing between them and begin to see how they dance together. Science and spirit are not in opposition; they complement one another in extraordinary ways.

Our brains function much like quantum computers, processing information through principles such as superposition and entanglement. Bits of data are constantly exchanged, giving us the ability to hold multiple realities at once—just as quantum particles do. This is the convergence of neuroscience, consciousness, and quantum theory. We are multidimensional beings, capable of processing more than we consciously understand.

Consider this: when we observe the world, we don't simply watch from the sidelines. Our observations affect outcomes. This is the infamous "spooky action at a distance" that Einstein described. Reality itself is fluid until we observe it; only then does it collapse into something definite. If infinite possibilities exist before observation, then consciousness is the key that turns possibility into form. This fusion of quantum theory with consciousness lies at the heart of the work we explore through Quantum Journeys Hypnosis™. Here, neuroscience, multidimensional awareness, and hypnotherapy meet—unlocking deeper levels of healing and transformation.

Our minds record and encode data from beliefs, narratives, and perceptions at the quantum level. That data shapes the very realities we live in. When we understand this, we gain the ability to heal, transform, and expand. We are not just spiritual beings. We are not just quantum processors. We are both. And it's time we embrace this truth.

When quantum theory blends with lived spirituality, we find ourselves equipped not only to meet the demands of physical reality but to reach into the infinite potential of multidimensional consciousness. As vast, non-corporeal beings in human form, we came here to interface between body, mind, and spirit—to weave intention into matter and become architects of our own realities.

Instead of being trapped in the Matrix, we discover that we are also the coders of it. Our thoughts, intentions, and emotions are not incidental; they are tools for shaping reality. Healing, manifestation, and higher states of awareness are not "metaphysical fluff." They may be written into the very structure of the universe.

Hypnosis and deep consciousness work provide portals into those liminal states where the boundaries between self and cosmos blur, where transformation becomes inevitable. Perhaps it is not just about shifting our individual realities, but also about interacting with dimensions, beings, and versions of ourselves that exist beyond the visible world. If this is true, then our familiar, linear, 3D reality is only a sliver of the picture. The work of awakening is not to escape it, but to see through it—realizing ourselves as multidimensional beings with endless access to possibility.

This anthology is a testament to that realization. Each story reflects not only the courage to explore inner landscapes, but also the willingness to remember that reality is far more fluid, interconnected, and astonishing than we have been led to believe. The future is not waiting for us. The future is quantum. And it's already here.

Acknowledgments

To the brilliant co-authors of *Quantum Journeys: Tales of Multidimensional Healing and Discovery*—thank you.

This book is not just a collection of stories; it is a chorus of voices, each carrying its own resonance of healing, courage, and discovery. By sharing your journeys, you've illuminated paths for others to follow, offering evidence that transformation is possible in ways both profound and unexpected.

Your contributions remind us that consciousness is vast and interconnected, and that when we step forward in trust, our stories ripple outward to touch lives we may never know. This second edition carries your light even further, expanding the reach of your words and the hope they inspire.

With deepest gratitude for your trust, wisdom, and willingness to be seen:

Carolyn Mather
Ruthie Ann Yielding
Christine Nicholson
Nikki Hoare
Persis Balsara-Wetzel

Tiani Lanet Perkins

Shelley Whister

Jonathan Finn

Cassidy Green

Henriette Kern-Schuh

Lorraine Dodder

Igor Vilusic

Joelle Anthony

Lisa Morgan

Terri Schmidt

Leslee Edmonson

Robyn Monteleone

Kryssa Marie Bowman

Sreshtha Tewari

Your stories are a gift to the world. Thank you for helping weave this tapestry of multidimensional healing and discovery.

~Kryssa

About the Author

Kryssa Marie Bowman lives and works in North Carolina, where she also spent a good portion of her early childhood-- after spending almost 3 decades in Montana, thus creating a closed loop...geographically speaking, anyway. She raised four incredible children, all of whom she is beyond proud of. Kryssa now spends her days facilitating hypnotherapy sessions, teaching Quantum Journeys Hypnosis, writing (adequately), gardening (poorly), meditating (exquisitely), and perfecting her feline language skills. She is also known to travel for live presentations at hypnosis conferences and events.

Reader's Notes: